THE NEW SIMPLY DELICIOUS

Rose Elliot is one of Britain's most famous writers on vegetarian cookery. She is the author of many best-selling books and her original and imaginative style has made her a favourite among vegetarians and non-vegetarians alike. Her recipes range from creations of subtle sophistication to simple and cheap dishes for the novice cook and those on a tight budget.

Rose Elliot became a cookery writer by accident. She was planning to take a degree in history when she met and married her husband and became involved in cooking, entertaining and bringing up a family. The original *Simply Delicious* was Rose's first cookery book. It met with immediate success, and launched Rose on her career. Rose tries out all her recipes at home, and the very best she includes in her books.

The New Simply Delicious

ROSE ELLIOT

Thorsons
An Imprint of HarperCollinsPublishers

Thorsons
An Imprint of HarperCollins*Publishers*
77–85 Fulham Palace Road,
Hammersmith, London W6 8JB
1160 Battery Street,
San Francisco, California 94111–1213

First published as *Simply Delicious*
by The White Eagle Publishing Trust 1967
Published by Fontana 1977, 1988
Published by Thorsons 1994
1 3 5 7 9 10 8 6 4 2

A catalogue record for this book
is available from the British Library

ISBN 0 7225 3042 0

Printed in Great Britain by
HarperCollinsManufacturing Glasgow

CONTENTS

PREFACE

I am specially pleased that Thorsons are republishing *Simply Delicious* in this new and attractive format. It was my first book and the one that launched my career as a cookery writer, although I had no idea of this nor ambition in that direction at the time. In my late teens I took over the cooking at a religious retreat centre run by my family in Hampshire, and I wrote *Simply Delicious* as a result of numerous requests for recipes. At that time (1967) there were very few vegetarian books available, and those that were tended to be rather wholesome but boring. Anyway, I think I must have tapped into a need because I was amazed at the favourable response, and all my other books have come about as a result.

It is difficult to be certain, but I sometimes wonder whether the increase in vegetarianism was triggered by my books, or whether the success of my books was due to the interest in vegetarianism: perhaps it was a bit of both. Anyway, *Simply Delicious* has been in print ever since, and I have followed it up with over 40 more vegetarian cookery books.

In 1988 I fully revised *Simply Delicious*, keeping the spirit of the book and its emphasis on fast, easy recipes for new vegetarians, but changing the format, updating the recipes and adding many new ones, together with notes on equipment, cooking processes and nutrition. The result is a book which is, I think, especially good for those who are either new to cookery or new to vegetarianism – or both! The emphasis is very much on speed; the food is health-giving and the kind that everyone likes, whether vegetarian or not. So if you are hesitating about eating or going vegetarian, I say give it a try and see for yourself. I think you will enjoy it.

AUTHOR'S NOTE

This is a completely new version of *Simply Delicious,* retaining the name and about a dozen of the original recipes. Everything else is appearing for the first time, but retains, I hope, the enthusiasm and simplicity which brought the first *Simply Delicious* so many friends.

Many recipes in this book can be ready for the table very quickly, in less than 15 minutes (extra quick), others in less than 40 minutes. These are marked in the recipes as shown below.

Other recipes can be prepared quickly, but may need to be chilled or cooked for a long period; this is noted at the beginning of the recipe and can be taken into account when planning meals.

◕ extra quick

◑ quick

Ⅴ indicates that the recipe is suitable for vegans: that is it contains no animal products (such as milk, butter, cheese, eggs), or offers vegan alternatives — e.g. margarine for butter, soya milk for cow's milk.

♀ indicates a special dish, suitable for a celebration or dinner party.

✳ at the bottom of a recipe indicates that the dish will freeze well.

1. Getting Started

Going vegetarian, or moving in that direction, is easy and fun. The food is healthy, delicious, simple to make and nothing like as strange as some people think. Indeed, many popular everyday dishes are in fact vegetarian: baked potatoes with cheese or soured cream, pizzas, quiches, omelette, spaghetti with tomato sauce, cheese soufflé, vegetable gratins, egg curry, fried eggs...

So begin by enjoying these favourite dishes, then gradually introduce new ones. As many of your favourite dishes are probably based on cheese or eggs, get variety and avoid having too much dairy produce by choosing dishes based on pulses, rice, nuts and vegetables — you will find plenty of easy ones in this book, as well as some interesting cheese and egg ones, to ring the changes.

A vegetarian meal can be planned just like a meat or fish one, simply swapping the meat or fish for a vegetarian dish. There's nothing complicated about it!

You will find details about ingredients, equipment, nutrition and meal-planning in the reference section of this book, pages 184–208. But in the meantime, you probably already have in your kitchen the equipment and ingredients to get you started, so my advice is to start right away with one of the snacks or extra quick dishes and go on from there. You'll not look back!

2. Snacks and Sandwiches

SNACKS

Baked Potatoes with Savoury Fillings ◷

Along with eggs, fresh fruit, cheese, nuts and raisins, potatoes are one of the great healthy convenience foods. Just scrub 1 large old potato per person, prick it several times with a fork, or cut a cross on the top. Then bake in a hot oven: 230°C/450°F/Gas Mark 8 for about 1 hour, or in a microwave on full power for 4–5 minutes for each potato. Whichever method you use, the potatoes are done when they feel soft when squeezed. Serve them with a knob of butter or margarine and/or any of these fillings:
— grated cheese
— cooked, drained sweetcorn
— soured cream and chopped chives — stir a tablespoonful of chopped fresh chives and some salt and pepper into a small carton of soured cream
— cooked, drained red kidney beans
— shredded lettuce and chopped tomato
— cottage cheese, plain or with chopped chives or spring onions

Egg and Cheese Snacks

Baked Egg ◐

Serves 1

1 egg
2 tablespoons cooked vegetables — onion, tomato, mushroom,
  ratatouille
salt and freshly ground black pepper
butter
small ovenproof dish or ramekin, well buttered

Preheat the oven to 180°C/350°F/Gas Mark 4.

Have ready a roasting tin and a kettle of boiling water. Put
the cooked vegetables into the ramekin, making a well in the
centre. Break in an egg, season with salt and pepper and dot
with a little butter. Place the ramekin in the roasting tin and
pour boiling water into the tin to come half way up the sides
of the ramekin. Cover the top of the ramekin with foil. Bake
for 10–12 minutes, until the egg is lightly set. Serve immediately.

Omelette ◐

The best frying pan to use for an omelette for one person is one measuring 12–15 cm/5–6 inches across the top; the ingredients can be doubled to make a two-person omelette, and in this case a larger frying pan is best, 25–26 cm/10 inches across.

Serves 1

2–3 eggs
salt and freshly ground black pepper
10 g (¼ oz) butter

Crack the eggs into a bowl, season with salt and pepper, and beat lightly, just to combine — don't beat them too much. Put the frying pan over a moderate to high heat for a minute or two, to heat up, then add the butter, so that it melts quickly without turning brown.

When the butter has melted and the froth has subsided, pour in the eggs. Stir the eggs gently with a fork, and as the bottom layer of egg begins to set draw it back with a spatula and tip the pan to allow the unset egg to run on to the hot pan. When the omelette is almost set — remember it will go on cooking in its own heat — arrange your chosen filling on top of it.

To fold the omelette and turn it out of the frying pan in one movement, hold the frying pan by its handle at right angles to the warmed plate. Using the spatula, roll the top third of the omelette down, and at the same time tip the frying pan over the plate, so that the omelette rolls and comes out of the pan simultaneously, landing on the plate folded side down. Serve immediately.

Blue Cheese Dip

This dip can be whizzed up quickly and, with toast or crudités, makes a good quick snack.

Serves 2

225 g (8 oz) cottage cheese
50 g (2 oz) Roquefort or other blue cheese
1 tablespoon milk, single cream or soured cream

Put all the ingredients into a liquidizer or blender and whizz to a smooth purée. Spoon into a small dish.

Cheesy Tomatoes

Big beefsteak tomatoes make the basis of a good quick snack.

Serves 2

1 large beefsteak tomato
50–100 g (2–4 oz) cheese, thinly sliced
a few crisp lettuce leaves
pieces of wholewheat toast

Preheat the grill. Slice the tomato into thick circles. Place these on the grill pan and arrange slices of cheese on top of the tomato. Grill until the cheese has melted and lightly browned. Serve on top of crisp lettuce leaves, accompanied by some fingers or triangles of wholewheat toast.

Bread and Toast Snacks

Garlic Bread ◖

This is generally served more as an accompaniment to soups, salads and dips than as a snack on its own, although when it comes out of the oven, crisp, hot and buttery, garlic bread is irresistible at any time.

Serves 6

1 French bread stick, white or wholewheat
2–3 garlic cloves, crushed
100 g (4 oz) butter, or margarine for vegans

Make slices in the French stick 2.5 cm/1 inch apart, cutting almost through so that the slices are still joined at the base. Beat the crushed garlic cloves into the butter or margarine and spread this on both sides of the slices of bread. Push the slices together to re-form the loaf, then wrap it in foil. Place on a baking tray and bake for about 20 minutes at 200°C/400°F/ Gas Mark 6 for about 20 minutes, until the bread has heated through and the butter melted. Serve immediately.

Cheese on Toast ◕

Serves 1

1–2 slices wholewheat bread
75–100 g (3–4 oz) cheese, grated
1–2 tablespoons milk
freshly ground black pepper

Heat the grill to high. Toast the bread on one side. Blend the cheese to a paste with the milk, and season with pepper. Spread the cheese mixture on the untoasted side of the bread and grill until puffed up and golden brown. Serve immediately.

Bap Pizzas ◑

Serves 1

1 wholewheat bap
1 large tomato, sliced
50–100 g (2–4 oz) cheese, grated
2–4 black olives (optional)

Heat the grill. Cut the bap in half and put the two halves on a grill pan. Arrange the tomato slices on top, pile the grated cheese on top of that, and arrange the olives on the cheese, if you're using them. Grill for a few minutes, until the cheese has melted and browned lightly. Serve immediately.

Vegetarian Burger Buns

You can use home-made nut burgers for these (perhaps from the freezer), see pages 76 and 79, or ready-made vegetarian burgers such as Vegeburgers.

Serves 1

1 wholewheat burger bun
oil
1 vegetarian burger, bought or home-made
   chutney, pickles or mustard to taste

Warm the burger bun under a moderate grill. Meanwhile, fry the burger in a little oil, then drain on kitchen paper. Split the burger bun, spread with a little chutney, pickle or mustard and place the burger on top. Cover with the other half of the bun and serve at once.

Toasted Sandwiches ◔ Ⓥ

You need a sandwich toaster to make these; one which automatically cuts the sandwiches in half and seals the edges gives the best results.

Serves 1

butter or margarine for spreading
2 pieces of wholewheat bread

Heat a sandwich toaster. Prepare your chosen filling — see below. Butter the bread on one side. Spread the unbuttered side with the filling and sandwich together. Toast for 4–5 minutes, until crisp and golden brown. Serve immediately.

Fillings for toasted sandwiches

Cheese
Grate or slice any firm cheese; or try a soft cheese, such as Brie, cream cheese, curd cheese or cottage cheese.

Bean
Mash cooked beans with a little of their liquid and any flavourings you fancy, such as crushed garlic, mustard, tomato purée, mayonnaise (for non-vegans) or chutney.

Salad Mix
Mix finely chopped or grated carrot, cauliflower, cabbage or spring onion with mayonnaise or soured cream to bind, or tofu dressing (page 201) for vegans.

Avocado
Mash a peeled avocado pear with a few drops of lemon juice and some salt and pepper to taste. Add a little chopped spring onion or crushed garlic if you like. Allow ½ large avocado pear or 1 small one for each sandwich.

Mushroom

Finely chop button mushrooms, allowing 125 g (4 oz) for each sandwich. Fry the mushrooms in a little butter, or oil or margarine for vegans, for 4–5 minutes, or longer if they make much liquid — cook them over a high heat until all the liquid has boiled away.

Egg

Put one of the slices of buttered bread on the sandwich toaster, buttered-side down; break an egg on the bread, then place the second slice of bread, on top, buttered-side up. Toast in the usual way, until the bread outside is crisp and brown, and the egg inside is set.

Filled Pitta Bread ◑

A pocket of pitta bread makes an excellent container: fill it with your choice of items such as shredded lettuce, sliced tomato, onion or avocado, cubes of cheese, nut roast or lentil roast; drained cooked or canned red kidney beans, cannellini beans or chick peas; or onion, cole slaw (page 111), bulgur wheat salad (page 118), or bean salad (page 119).

Serves 4

4 wholewheat pitta breads
4–8 lettuce leaves, shredded
425 g (15 oz) can chick peas, drained
1 small onion, peeled and cut into thin rings (optional)
125 g (4 oz) firm cheese, cut into small dice

Slit each pitta bread at the top and ease open, to make a pocket for the filling. Mix together the lettuce, chick peas, onion and cheese, then fill the pitta breads with this mixture, dividing it between them.

Filled French Bread

This can be prepared very quickly, but needs to be chilled.

Serves 4

2 wholewheat French bread sticks
butter or mayonnaise, or margarine or mustard for vegans
1 lettuce, washed and shredded
225 g (8 oz) tomatoes, sliced
100 g (4 oz) beansprouts
1 onion, peeled and sliced
425 g (15 oz) can red kidney beans, drained
salt and freshly ground black pepper

Make a slit down the side of each French stick and scoop
out a little of the crumb. Spread the inside of each French
loaf thinly with butter, mayonnaise, margarine, or mustard.
Fill each loaf with the vegetables and beans, and season with
salt and pepper. Press the slits together, wrap the loaves tightly
in foil and chill until required, then cut each in half.

SANDWICHES ◔ Ⓥ

There's no doubt that a sandwich makes one of the quickest and most satisfactory snacks or light meals. You can introduce variety by using different types of bread such as light-textured wholewheat, heavy-textured wholewheat, rye, or granary. There are plenty of fillings which do not contain meat or fish. Here are some suggestions, starting with everyday lunch-box fillers and ending with a few extravaganzas for when you feel like making a very special sandwich.

Sandwich Fillings

—yeast extract, miso, peanut butter or sesame spread for vegans, or curd or cream cheese or salad cream, with cucumber, lettuce, beansprouts, tomato or grated carrot
—curd or cream cheese with finely chopped nuts or dates
—mashed cooked red kidney beans with salad
—chopped hard-boiled egg mixed with salad cream or milk, or scrambled egg, with cress
—grated carrot mixed with mayonnaise (or tofu dressing for vegans) and chopped herbs or raisins
—sliced or grated cheese with lettuce, tomato or cucumber
—sliced banana, with or without peanut butter or sesame spread
—honey and finely ground nuts
—Cheddar cheese and chutney
—cream cheese or curd cheese with chopped herbs or chopped nuts
—cream cheese, chopped preserved ginger or dates and chopped walnuts
—yeast extract and wafer-thin cucumber slices
—finely grated cheese blended with cream, milk or curd cheese
—thinly sliced nut roast or lentil roast, with sliced tomato and mayonnaise, or horseradish sauce or chutney, for non-vegans.
—Tartex vegetable pâté and sliced cucumber

19

—hummus with a little black olive pâté
—scrambled egg with cooked asparagus tips
—sliced lettuce hearts, Brie, sliced avocado and chopped walnuts
—shredded lettuce, sliced canned artichoke hearts, mayonnaise, watercress and toasted pine kernels

Sandwiches will freeze as long as they don't contain hardboiled egg, mayonnaise or salad vegetables.

3. Soups and Starters

SOUPS

Making soup is quick and easy, and the results are delicious. No complicated techniques are involved, no hours of stock-making. It helps if you have a liquidizer or food processor if you want a smooth soup, although many mixtures are equally good served un-liquidized.

As far as stock is concerned, you can make a good vegetarian one by simmering an onion, carrot, a few celery sticks, a bay leaf, a sprig of thyme and some parsley stalks in plenty of water for a couple of hours, then straining. However I rarely do this. I prefer the clear flavour which ordinary water gives to a vegetable-based soup; for a more intense flavour, I sometimes use a good-quality vegetarian stock powder or concentrate. Marigold Bouillon powder is particularly good, as is a Swiss concentrate called Hügli.

A soup can make a delicious light meal if served with crusty bread and perhaps some good cheese, with salad or fresh fruit.

Tomato Soup ◑ Ⅴ

A quick and popular soup

Serves 4

1 onion, peeled and chopped
15 g (½ oz) butter or margarine
350 g (12 oz) potatoes, peeled and diced
450 g (1 lb) tomatoes, skinned and sliced, or 400 g can tomatoes
900 ml (1½ pints) vegetable stock or water
salt and freshly ground black pepper

Fry the onion in the butter or margarine in a large saucepan, covered, for 5 minutes, without browning. Add the potatoes, cover again and cook gently for a further 5–10 minutes, then add the tomatoes and cook for a further 4–5 minutes. Stir from time to time and do not allow the vegetables to brown. Add the stock or water, cover the pan and leave the soup to simmer for 15–20 minutes, until the potatoes are tender.

   Purée the soup in a blender or food processor and, if you want it really smooth, sieve it to remove the tomato seeds (this is not essential). Reheat the soup gently without boiling.

Watercress Soup ◑ ♀

This soup is very good hot, and, in warm weather, it's equally delicious served well chilled. To make a smooth soup, you really need a liquidizer or food processor, although you could manage without if you mash the potato pieces in the soup with a spoon and finely chop the watercress before adding it.

Serves 4

1 onion, peeled and chopped
15 g (½ oz) butter or margarine
700 g (1½ lb) potatoes, peeled and diced
900 ml (1½ pints) vegetable stock or water
1 bunch of watercress
salt and freshly ground black pepper
3–4 tablespoons double cream

Fry the onion in the butter or margarine in a large saucepan, covered, for 5 minutes, without browning. Add the potatoes, cover again and cook gently for a further 5–10 minutes. Stir from time to time and do not allow the vegetables to brown. Stir in the stock or water and leave the soup to simmer for about 20 minutes, until the potatoes are tender.

Liquidize the soup with the watercress. Reheat without boiling, season to taste with salt and pepper and stir in the cream.

Lentil Soup Ⓥ

One of the best and most popular of vegetarian soups, nourishing and easy to make.

Serves 4–6

1 large onion, peeled and chopped
15 g (½ oz) butter or margarine
225 g (8 oz) red lentils
1 litre (1¾ pints) vegetable stock or water
1–2 teaspoons lemon juice
salt and freshly ground black pepper

Fry the onion in the butter or margarine in a saucepan or pressure-cooker pan for 10 minutes, until it is soft but has not browned. Add the lentils and stir for 1–2 minutes, then add the stock or water. Bring to the boil, then half cover the pan and leave the soup to simmer gently for 20 minutes, until the lentils are very tender and pale-coloured. Or cook in a pressure-cooker for 5 minutes.

Beat the soup with a spoon to break up the lentils and make it smoother, or purée in a blender or food processor. Add the lemon juice and salt and pepper to taste.

✳

Leek and Potato Soup ◑ Ⓥ

Serves 4–6

3 leeks, washed and sliced
700 g (1½ lb) potatoes, peeled and diced
25 g (1 oz) butter or margarine
1 litre (1¾ pints) vegetable stock or water
3–4 tablespoons double cream (optional)
Salt and freshly ground black pepper
1–2 tablespoons chopped parsley (optional)

Fry the leeks and potatoes very gently in the butter or margarine in a large saucepan, covered, for 10 minutes, stirring often. Cook gently without browning, still covered, for a further 10 minutes, stirring from time to time to prevent the vegetables sticking to the pan. Add the stock or water, stir, then simmer for 5–10 minutes, until the vegetables are tender.

Purée in a blender or food processor, adding the cream if using. Season to taste with salt and pepper, stir, and serve in warmed bowls. Sprinkle with chopped parsley, if wished.

Mushroom and Sea Vegetable Soup ◐ Ⓥ

This is a pleasant soup with a taste of the sea. It is also nourishing, because wakame is a rich source of calcium and iron. You can buy wakame at some health food shops and stockists of Japanese and Chinese foods.

Serves 4

3–4 pieces of wakame
65 g (2½ oz) butter or margarine
1 onion, peeled and chopped
450 g (1 lb) button mushrooms, washed and sliced
1 litre (1¾ pints) water
2 teaspoons vegetarian stock powder
50 g (2 oz) wholewheat flour
2–3 tablespoons chopped parsley
salt and freshly ground black pepper

Wash the wakame, then cover it with water and leave to soften for a few minutes. Once the wakame becomes flexible, remove and discard the central spine and any other stems and chop the wakame. Melt 15 g (½ oz) of the butter or margarine in a saucepan and fry the onion for 5 minutes, then add the mushrooms and fry for a further 2–3 minutes. Put in the wakame, water and stock powder and bring to the boil.

Meanwhile, melt the rest of the butter or margarine in a large saucepan and add the flour. Stir for a moment or two, then gradually add the mushroom mixture, stirring all the time until thickened. Leave the soup to simmer gently for about 10 minutes, to cook the flour, then add the parsley and some salt and pepper to taste.

Chilled Cucumber Soup ◑ ♀

This chilled soup makes a beautifully refreshing start to a special summer meal.

Serves 4

1 large cucumber
1 small onion
900 ml (1½ pints) vegetable stock or water
4 good sprigs of mint
2 teaspoons cornflour or arrowroot
150 ml (5 fl oz) single cream
salt and freshly ground black pepper
chopped mint to garnish

Peel the cucumber thinly and cut into small pieces; peel and chop the onion. Put the cucumber and onion into a saucepan with the water or vegetable stock and the sprigs of mint. Bring to the boil, then cover and simmer for about 10 minutes, until the cucumber and onion are tender. Remove the mint sprigs.

Liquidize the soup and return it to the pan. Put the cornflour or arrowroot into a small bowl and blend to a paste with half the cream. Pour this mixture into the saucepan, stirring all the time. Bring to the boil and cook for a few seconds until thickened, then remove from the heat. Season with salt and pepper.

Let the soup get cold, then chill it in the fridge until you are ready to eat. Check the seasoning, then serve the soup in chilled bowls, with the rest of the cream and a scattering of chopped mint on top.

SIMPLE STARTERS

It's always helpful, when you're entertaining, to be able to make the starter, and perhaps the pudding, too, in advance, so that you can give all your attention to the main course and enjoy more of the company of your guests.

The starters in this section are all useful in this respect, and make an easy, mouth-watering start to any special meal.

Hummus ◐ Ⓥ

This delectable, creamy dip is quick and easy to make in a liquidizer or food processor. It looks particularly attractive when arranged in the traditional manner described. Serve with strips of warmed pitta bread or crudités (see below).

Serves 4

425 g (15 oz) can chick peas
½ garlic clove, crushed
1 tablespoon light sesame cream
3 tablespoons olive oil

2 tablespoons lemon juice
salt and freshly ground black pepper

To garnish

olive oil
paprika pepper (optional)
lemon wedges
black olives

Drain the chick peas, reserving the liquid. Put the chick peas into a blender or food processor with all the other ingredients and blend until the mixture is smooth. Alternatively, mash the chick peas as smoothly as possible and then beat in the other ingredients to make a smoothish mixture. Add enough of the reserved cooking liquid to give a light, soft consistency like softly whipped cream.

Spoon the hummus on to a plate and level it with a knife so that it is about 1 cm/½ inch deep. Pour a little olive oil over the top, then sprinkle with paprika, if using, and garnish with lemon wedges and olives.

✱ If freezing hummus, add the garlic just before serving.

27

Crudités

This colourful assortment of vegetables is ideal for serving with dips, or makes a refreshing pre-meal nibble at any time. They also make a good snack for children (or others!) — my youngest daughter, Claire, loves a little basket of crudités with a pot of cottage cheese or a little mayonnaise to dip them in.

Choose really crisp, fresh vegetables in contrasting colours and flavours. Have at least three different types, arranged in little heaps on a leaf-lined plate or tray, or pile them up in a small basket with the dips arranged around the outside. Some possibilities are:

— ruby-red radishes, with the root trimmed but the leaves left on
— spring onions, trimmed
— matchsticks of scraped carrot
— matchsticks of crisp celery
— matchsticks of red, green or yellow pepper, or cucumber
— sprigs of cauliflower – especially good for scooping up dips
— crisp chicory leaves
— large juicy black olives
— cherry tomatoes
— baby button mushrooms
— mangetout peas, topped and tailed

Avocado Dip ◑ ♀

This is a version of the classic guacamole, and the addition of the chilli gives it quite a bite: add it little by little, or leave it out if you prefer a gentler flavour. When cutting the chilli, do so carefully and don't touch your face, especially your eyes, until you have washed your hands thoroughly, because the juice can cause irritations. Serve with crisps, tortilla chips or crudités (see opposite page).

Serves 6

2 ripe avocado pears, halved, peeled and stones removed
2 tablespoons lemon or fresh lime juice
1 small onion, peeled
2 tomatoes, skinned and de-seeded
1 garlic clove, peeled
1 small green chilli pepper, de-seeded
a few coriander or parsley sprigs
salt and freshly ground black pepper
a little mild paprika pepper (optional)

Mash the avocado with the lemon or lime juice, then finely chop the rest of the ingredients and add, mixing well. Check the seasoning, then spoon the mixture into a small bowl, smooth the top and sprinkle with a little mild paprika pepper, for a touch of contrasting colour, if you like.

Tsatsiki ◑

This Greek cucumber dip makes a pleasant starter, accompanied by warm pitta bread or crudités (page 28); or it can be served as part of a salad meal. It's excellent, too, served with hot crisp burgers or falafel.

Serves 4

1 large cucumber, peeled and cut into 5 mm/¼ inch dice
salt
200 g (7 oz) carton Greek yogurt, strained
1 garlic clove, peeled and crushed
1 tablespoon chopped fresh mint
freshly ground black pepper
a few crisp lettuce leaves
4 black olives
4 fresh mint sprigs

Put the cucumber pieces into a colander, sprinkle with a little salt, place a plate and a weight on top, and leave for about 30 minutes, to remove excess liquid. Then pat the cucumber dry with kitchen paper and place in a bowl. Add the yogurt, garlic, mint and salt and pepper to taste.

Chill until needed, then serve on individual plates, spooning the cucumber mixture on to a base of crisp lettuce leaves and garnishing each with a black olive and mint sprig.

Pears with Tarragon Cream ◑ ♀

Choosing really good pears makes all the difference to this delicious starter; I generally buy them when they're hard, up to a week in advance, and allow them to ripen at room temperature, so that they're just right. They should be ripe enough to slice like butter with a fork, but not over-ripe. For a balanced meal, don't serve fruit or cream in the other courses.

Serves 6

150 ml (5 fl oz) double cream
1 tablespoon tarragon vinegar
caster sugar, salt and freshly ground black pepper
3 large ripe dessert pears, preferably Comice
2 tablespoons lemon juice
12 lettuce leaves
mild paprika pepper
6 tarragon sprigs

First make the tarragon cream. Put the cream into a bowl with the vinegar, a pinch each of sugar and salt and a grinding of black pepper, and whisk until thick but still soft and floppy. Taste and add a little more sugar, salt and pepper if needed, then chill until required.

Just before you want to serve the meal, halve and peel the pears, and carefully remove the cores — a teaspoon is good for doing this. Brush the pears all over with lemon juice. Put two lettuce leaves on each plate and place a pear, core-side down, on top. Spoon the cream on top of the pears, dividing it between them, then sprinkle a little paprika pepper on top of each, and garnish with a fresh tarragon sprig if you have any. Serve at once.

Avocado, Orange and Grapefuit Ⓥ ♀

One of the prettiest and most refreshing starters.

Serves 4–6

3 avocado pears
2 tablespoons lemon juice
1 large grapefruit
2 large oranges
sugar
½ bunch watercress

Cut the avocado pears in half and remove the stones and skin. Slice the avocados into pieces and put into a bowl with the lemon juice. Hold the grapefruit over the bowl and peel it by cutting the peel off with a sharp knife, along with the white pith, peeling round and round like you would an apple if you wanted to keep the piece of peel intact. Then cut the segments of flesh away from the transparent skin. When all the segments have been removed, squeeze the skin over the bowl to extract all the juice. Peel and segment the oranges in the same way. Taste the mixture and sweeten with a little sugar if necessary. Serve on individual plates or bowls and garnish with sprigs of fresh watercress.

Vegetables À La Grecque Ⓥ ♀

Any selection of vegetables can be used to make this delicious starter, but don't repeat the same vegetables in the next course; serve with warm rolls or French bread. The preparation is quick but the finished dish needs to be chilled.

Serves 4

225 g (8 oz) French beans, topped, tailed and cut into 2.5 cm/1 inch lengths
1 small cauliflower, divided into florets
4 tablespoons olive oil
1 tablespoon coriander seeds, roughly crushed with a pestle and mortar or with the back of a teaspoon
2 bay leaves
1 garlic clove, peeled and crushed
125 g (4 oz) button mushrooms, washed, and any larger ones halved or quartered
2 tablespoons lemon juice
salt and freshly ground black pepper
1–2 tablespoons chopped fresh parsley

Cook the French beans and cauliflower in 2.5 cm/1 inch boiling water in a pan for 2–3 minutes, to soften them slightly. Drain immediately, rinse under cold water, drain and pat dry on kitchen paper.

Heat the olive oil in a large frying pan or saucepan, add the coriander seeds, bay leaves, garlic and mushrooms and fry for 1–2 minutes, then add the beans and cauliflower and stir over the heat for a further 2–3 minutes. Remove from the heat and add the lemon juice and some salt and pepper to taste. Cool, then transfer to a bowl and chill. Serve on individual plates, sprinkled with chopped parsley.

Garlic Mushrooms ◐ ♀

These are served hot, so need some last-minute attention, although all the main preparation can be done in advance. Serve warm bread or rolls with them to mop up the buttery juices.

Serves 4

450 g (1 lb) button mushrooms
50 g (2 oz) butter or margarine
1–2 large garlic cloves, peeled and crushed
salt and freshly ground black pepper

The mushrooms should be roughly the same size, so halve or quarter any larger ones. Wash the mushrooms quickly, then dry them on kitchen paper and leave them on one side until just before you want to eat.

Have four deep individual dishes or soup bowls warm, ready to put the mushrooms in when they are ready.

Heat the butter or margarine in a large saucepan or frying pan, and when it's hot but not browned, put in the mushrooms and garlic. Stir all the time over the heat, for about 3–4 minutes, until the mushrooms are hot and beginning to get tender, but don't let them get to the stage where they produce lots of water. (If this does happen, drain the liquid off and add a bit more butter and garlic).

Spoon the mushrooms into the four bowls and serve immediately.

4. Easy Main Meals

Vegetarian main dishes are made from beans, lentils, rice or other grains, pasta, pastry, cheese, eggs, vegetables and nuts.

One of these main dishes can take the place of a meat or fish dish, and is served with cooked vegetables or a salad. It's a good idea to serve a main meal from a different section each day, to vary the protein sources and make sure that you don't over-emphasize the dairy proteins.

BEAN AND LENTIL DISHES

Beans and lentils are a cheap and healthy source of protein and can be made into some tasty and warming dishes.

I have used split red lentils in these recipes, because they are widely available, cook quickly without soaking and are, in my opinion, particularly delicious.

Red kidney beans and chick peas also feature and you can use either canned or dried ones.

If you are using dried beans, cover them with plenty of cold water and either soak overnight, or bring them to the boil, for 2 minutes, then remove from the heat, cover and leave for 1 hour. Then, in either case, drain and rinse the beans and put them into a saucepan with enough water to cover them. Bring to the boil, and boil vigorously for 10 minutes, then lower the heat and leave the beans to simmer for about 45 minutes, or until the beans are tender. Sometimes chick peas take a very long time — as much as 2–3 hours.

Dried beans and lentils can also be cooked in a pressure cooker. Soak them first as described, then follow the instructions given with your pressure cooker. Or put the beans into the pressure cooker, cover with their height again in water, bring up to pressure, and cook for about 20 minutes, or until tender. Cooked beans can be frozen; it's a good idea to cook 500 g (1 lb) at a time, then divide them into five equal portions (which are each equivalent to the contents of a 425 g (15 oz) can) and freeze them in polythene bags.

Easy Lentil Stew ◑ Ⓥ

Simple, cheap and warming, this is good served with something crisp, like garlic bread (page 14), warm crusty rolls, crunchy jacket potatoes or roast potatoes. The quantities can be quartered or halved to serve one or two people, but any extra mixture freezes well.

Serves 4

2 tablespoons vegetable oil
1 large onion, peeled and chopped
175 g (6 oz) red lentils
450 g (1 lb) mixed root vegetables such as celery, carrot, leek, swede, prepared, peeled and cut into even-sized chunks, or a 450 g (1 lb) bag of frozen casserole vegetables
1 garlic clove, peeled and crushed
425 g (15 oz) can tomatoes
900 ml (1½ pints) water
1 heaped teaspoon vegetarian stock powder
salt and freshly ground black pepper
125 g (4 oz) frozen peas
125 g (4 oz) button mushrooms, washed and sliced

Heat the oil in a large saucepan, then add the onion and fry over a moderate heat for 10 minutes, stirring from time to time. Put the lentils into a sieve and wash them quickly under the cold tap, then add them to the saucepan, along with the prepared vegetables and the garlic. Stir over the heat for a couple of minutes, to mix everything together, then add the tomatoes, water, stock powder and a seasoning of salt and pepper. Bring up to the boil, then put a lid on the pan and turn the heat down so that the mixture just simmers. Leave to cook for about 15 minutes, until the vegetables and lentils are nearly tender, then add the frozen peas and mushrooms and cook for a further 5–10 minutes, when the vegetables should be done and the lentils soft and pale. Check the seasoning, then serve.

Lentil Gratin

Another very easy, economical dish, this is good served with a salad or with a cooked vegetable such as green beans, sprouts, cabbage or spinach. Cook it in a big shallow casserole so that there is plenty of crunchy topping.

Serves 4

25 g (1 oz) butter or 2 tablespoons vegetable oil
2 onions, peeled and chopped
2 large carrots, scraped and cut into 5 mm/¼ inch dice
2 large celery sticks, trimmed and cut into 5 mm/¼ inch dice
225 g (8 oz) red lentils
600 ml (1 pint) water
salt and freshly ground black pepper
100 g (4 oz) Cheddar cheese, grated
3–4 heaped tablespoons wholewheat crumbs, dry or fresh
shallow casserole (or roasting tin), approximately 19 × 29 cm/7½ × 11½ inches, well-buttered

Heat the butter or oil in a large saucepan, then add the onion, carrot and celery, stir briefly, then put a lid on the pan and leave over a moderate heat for 10 minutes, stirring from time to time. Put the lentils into a sieve and wash them quickly under the cold tap, then add them to the saucepan and stir to distribute all the ingredients. Add the water and a seasoning of salt and pepper. Bring to the boil, then put a lid on the pan and turn the heat down so that the mixture just simmers. Leave to cook for 25–30 minutes, until the vegetables are tender and the lentils soft and pale. Check the seasoning, then turn the mixture into the prepared shallow casserole and sprinkle the cheese and breadcrumbs on top. All this can be done well in advance, and then the casserole can be baked for 30–40 minutes in the oven at 180°C/350°F/Gas Mark 4. Or, if you want to serve it straight away, make sure that the lentil mixture is piping hot when you put it into the casserole and just finish it off by putting it under a hot grill to melt the grated cheese and brown the breadcrumbs.

⁂ Freeze before giving the casserole its final grilling.

Vegetarian Chilli ◐ Ⓥ

Another recipe that's really quick to make. It's good served with baked potatoes split with soured cream and chopped chives in them; or with some mashed potatoes or fluffy brown rice and perhaps a quick green salad.

Serves 4

2 tablespoons olive oil
2 medium onions, peeled and chopped
1 red pepper, de-seeded and sliced
1 green pepper, de-seeded and sliced
2 × 425 g (15 oz) can red kidney beans, or 225 g (8 oz)
    dried red kidney beans, soaked and cooked (page 35)
1 garlic clove, peeled and crushed
425 g (15 oz) can tomatoes
½ teaspoon hot chilli powder
salt and freshly ground black pepper

Heat the oil in a large saucepan, add the onion and stir. Cover and leave to cook over a moderate heat for 5 minutes, stirring occasionally. Then add the peppers and cook for a further 5 minutes. Next drain the beans and add to the mixture, together with the garlic, tomatoes, chilli and a seasoning of salt and pepper. Bring to a gentle simmer, then cook for about 20 minutes, stirring from time to time.

Stir in the chilli when you reheat the mixture for serving.

Dal V

A simple recipe for this spicy lentil mixture, based on the one given in Rosamund Richardson's *Gourmet Vegetarian Cooking* published by Sainsbury's. It is good served with plain or spiced rice, or as a side dish with a vegetable curry; or, if you're watching the calories, try it spooned over lightly-cooked cabbage, accompanied by sliced tomatoes and sprinkled lightly with desiccated coconut. The dal can be made in 30–40 minutes but is best left to stand for 20–30 minutes, to allow the flavours to develop.

Serves 4

225 g (8 oz) red lentils
1 onion, peeled and sliced
1 bay leaf
1 whole fresh green chilli
2 cm/1 inch fresh ginger, peeled and grated
1 teaspoon turmeric
1–2 teaspoons salt
2 teaspoons ground cumin
2 teaspoons ground coriander

Put the lentils into a medium-sized saucepan with the onion, bay leaf, chilli, ginger, turmeric, and enough cold water just to cover. Bring to the boil, then cover and simmer very gently for 20–30 minutes, or until the lentils and onion are tender. Remove from the heat, stir in the salt, cumin and coriander, and leave to stand, covered, for a further 20–30 minutes for the flavours to develop. Mix with a wooden spoon to mash the lentils a little: the mixture should be thick and purée-like, but not stodgy, in texture. Reheat gently and serve.

Lentil Roast

This is an extremely simple roast made from red lentils; it has a delicate flavour. Like the nut roast, it makes a vegetarian replacement for a roast; serve it with all the traditional accompaniments, such as gravy, bread sauce, roast potatoes and some cooked vegetables such as carrots and cabbage. It's also particularly good cold, because it slices well, and is delicious with a sweet chutney or pickle, or some yogurt or mayonnaise, perhaps spiced by stirring in a few pinches of curry powder.

Serves 4

350 g (12 oz) red lentils
400 ml (15 fl oz) water
25 g (1 oz) butter or margarine
1 large onion, peeled and finely chopped
1 teaspoon mixed dried herbs
125 g (4 oz) cheese, grated
1 tablespoon lemon juice
1 egg, beaten
a few soft or dried breadcrumbs
salt and freshly ground black pepper
flour to coat
oil

Put the lentils into a saucepan with the water, bring to the boil, then turn the heat right down, cover, and cook for 20–25 minutes, until the lentils are soft, pale-coloured and all the water has been absorbed.

While this is happening, melt the butter or margarine in a large saucepan and fry the onion for 10 minutes, over a fairly gentle heat, with a lid on the pan. Stir from time to time, allowing the onion to brown a bit.

Set the oven to 190°C/375°F/Gas Mark 5.

Add the onion to the lentils together with the mixed herbs, cheese, lemon juice and beaten egg. Mix well, adding a few breadcrumbs to the mixture if necessary to stiffen it. Season

41

with salt and freshly ground black pepper. Sprinkle some flour on a board, turn the lentil mixture onto this, then use your hands to form the lentil mixture into a roll shape, coating it well with the flour.

Cover the base of a baking tin with 6 mm/¼ inch of oil and heat in the oven for about 4 minutes, or until the oil is smoking hot, then carefully put the lentil roll into the tin and spoon a little of the oil over it. Put it in the oven and bake for about 45 minutes, or until the roast is browned and crisp all over. Baste (spoon some of the oil over the roast) every 15 minutes or so, if possible.

Lift the roast out of the tin by placing a fish slice under one end and another fish slice or a palette knife under the other. Place on a warmed serving dish.

✳ Can be frozen either before or after cooking.

Falafel ◑

These are tasty chick pea rissoles from the Middle East, with a crisp coating on the outside. I think the nicest way to serve them is Middle Eastern fashion, with several bowls of salads and dips and some warmed pitta bread; everyone can take a scoop of whatever they fancy, dipping the falafel into the dips before eating. Suggestions are tomato and onion salad, hummus, cucumber and yogurt dip, a green salad made with shredded lettuce, pretty carrot salad. I think they are nicest when deep-fried, but it's often easier, rather than using a large deep-frier, just to heat 5 cm/2 inches of oil in a heavy-based medium saucepan and fry the falafel in two or three batches.

Serves 4

2 × 400 g (14 oz) cans chick peas
50 g (2 oz) peeled onion
1 garlic clove, peeled
4 good sprigs mint, or 1 teaspoon mint sauce concentrate
4–6 sprigs parsley
salt and freshly ground black pepper
flour
2 eggs, beaten
100 g (4 oz) dried wholewheat crumbs
oil for deep-frying

Drain the chick peas, saving the liquid. If you are using a food processor, cut the onion into chunks, remove and discard any tough stems from the mint and parsley; put into the food processor with the chick peas and whole garlic clove and whizz to a thick purée. Without a food processor, mash the chick peas well, chop the onion very finely or grate it, crush the garlic and chop the mint and parsley. Then mix together the chick peas, onion, garlic, mint and parsley.

Season the chick pea mixture, then divide it into eight even-sized pieces and dip each first in flour then in egg and dried breadcrumbs. Form into rounds, like golf balls.

Heat the oil. Test it by putting in a cube of bread, and if it sizzles and rises to the surface immediately, then begins to turn golden brown, the oil is ready for frying. Put in the falafel and fry them for 4–5 minutes, until they are deep brown and crisp all over. Remove them with a perforated spoon and drain on crumpled kitchen paper. Serve hot, or warm.
[✳] Freeze before frying, then fry, gently from frozen; or freeze after frying, for reheating in the microwave.

RICE DISHES

Brown rice is a wholesome ingredient, rich in fibre and containing useful amounts of protein, minerals and B vitamins. It can be made into some very good vegetarian main courses. The type of brown rice which is widely available is long grain and this is suitable for all savoury dishes with the exception of risotto (page 52), for which a round-grain rice is needed as this breaks up and becomes creamy. Italian Arborio rice (which isn't brown) is the best to use for risotto; you can get it from Italian shops and Sainsbury's. Alternatively, you could use a round-grain or short-grain brown rice from the health food shop, or a white short-grain, round-grain, 'pudding' or Carolina rice from any supermarket.

Basmati rice is a specially delicate rice from a particular area of India. Both brown and white varieties are available; it cooks more quickly than ordinary rice.

Basic Cooking of Rice

There are two basic methods of cooking rice, both equally good.

For the absorption method put one measure of rice into a heavy-based saucepan with two measures of water and a little salt; bring to the boil, then put a lid on the pan and cook over the lowest possible heat until all the water has been absorbed and the rice is tender. This takes 40–45 minutes for ordinary brown rice, about 20 minutes for white rice. In this method, flavourings can be added to the pan, as in the spiced rice recipe on page 48. The rice can also be fried in a little butter or oil before the water is put in (see below).

For the immersion method bring a large panful of water to the boil then put in the rice, bring back to the boil and let the mixture boil away until a grain of rice, retrieved with a slotted spoon, feels tender. This takes about 25–30 minutes for brown rice, 12–15 minutes for white rice. Basmati rice, both white and brown, takes a few minutes less as it is slimmer.

Basic Brown Rice ☑

Serves 4

25 g (1 oz) butter or 2 tablespoons olive oil
225 g (8 oz) long grain brown rice
1 teaspoon salt
600 ml (1 pint) water

Melt half the butter or oil in a medium saucepan, then add the rice and fry for 3–4 minutes, stirring all the time. Then add the salt and water. Bring to the boil, then turn the heat right down, put a lid on the pan, and leave the rice to cook for 40–45 minutes. Add the rest of the butter or oil and mix it gently into the rice with a fork.

Vegetable Curry and Brown Rice ☑

This is a very pleasant English-style curry, delicious with some buttered brown rice and side dishes of sliced tomatoes with raw onion rings, and salted peanuts or cashew nuts. If you can't get whole coriander seeds, these can be left out, but they do give a particularly pleasant delicate burnt-orange taste, and crunchy texture, different from ready-ground coriander.

Serves 4

225 g (8 oz) brown rice
salt

For the curry

225 g (8 oz) leeks, trimmed, leaving up to 5 cm/2 inches of the green leaves on, if good, then cleaned thoroughly and cut into 2 cm/1 inch pieces
1 small cauliflower, divided into florets
1 onion, peeled and chopped
225 g (8 oz) potatoes, cut into even-sided pieces
1 small cooking apple, peeled and chopped

1 heaped tablespoon plain wholewheat flour
1 tablespoon turmeric powder
2 teaspoons curry powder
4 tablespoons vegetable oil
225 g (8 oz) can tomatoes
300 ml (½ pint) water
1 teaspoon whole coriander seeds, coarsely crushed with a
    pestle and mortar, rolling pin or back of a teaspoon
3 rounded tablespoons mango chutney, large pieces chopped
salt and freshly ground black pepper

First of all, get the rice on to cook, as it will take about
45 minutes (unless you use a pressure-cooker — for this allow
10 minutes under pressure, then allow pressure to reduce
naturally). Put the rice into a heavy-based saucepan with a
little salt and 600 ml (1 pint) of water and bring to the boil.
Then put a lid on the pan, turn the heat down as low as
possible and leave the rice to cook for 40–45 minutes.

While the rice is cooking, make the curry. Put all the
vegetables and the apple into a large bowl and sprinkle with
the flour, turmeric and curry powder. Mix well, so that the
flour and turmeric are well distributed. Next put the oil into
a large saucepan and when it's hot, put in the vegetable and
flour mixture. Mix well and fry lightly, stirring often, for
about 5 minutes. Then add the tomatoes, water, crushed
coriander seeds, mango chutney, some salt and pepper. Mix
gently, bring to the boil, then put a lid on the pan and simmer
gently for 30 minutes. Check the seasoning and serve.

Spiced Vegetables and Saffron Rice Ⓥ ♀

One of my favourite recipes, this curry has an authentic
flavour.

Serves 4

For the rice

225 g (8 oz) Basmati rice
1½ tablespoons olive oil
1 onion, peeled and finely chopped
6 strands of saffron (optional)
4 black peppercorns
1 clove
2 cardamom pods, lightly crushed with a teaspoon or
  rolling pin
½ cinnamon stick
400 ml (15 fl oz) water
1 teaspoon salt

For the spiced vegetables

120 ml (6 fl oz) olive oil
1 teaspoon white mustard seeds
½ teaspoon turmeric
14 curry leaves, lightly chopped, or if not available,
  ½ teaspoon curry powder
4 garlic cloves, peeled and crushed
4 cm/1½ inches fresh ginger, peeled and grated
¼ teaspoon hot chilli powder
1 medium cauliflower, broken into florets, to make
  700 g (1½ lb)
100 g (4 oz) green beans, trimmed and cut into
  2 cm/1 inch lengths
225 g (8 oz) carrots, scraped and cut into 5 mm/¼ inch rounds
8 leaves of spinach or cabbage, washed and roughly chopped
salt and freshly ground black pepper

Start by preparing the rice. Put the rice into a sieve and wash under the cold tap until the water runs clear. Shake the sieve well to get rid of as much water as possible, then leave on one side to drain. Heat the oil in a medium-sized heavy-based saucepan and add the onion; fry over a gentle heat, with a lid on the pan, for 5 minutes, then add all the spices and stir over the heat for a further 1–2 minutes. Add the rice, mix well, then add the water and salt. Bring up to the boil, then put a lid on the pan, reduce the heat, and leave to cook gently for 20 minutes.

Meanwhile, make the spiced vegetables. Put the oil into a large saucepan and heat. When it is hot, put in the mustard seeds — they should sizzle immediately — the turmeric, curry leaves, garlic, ginger and chilli. Fry for 2 minutes, but don't let the spices burn. Then put in the cauliflower, beans and carrots. Mix well, then cover and cook gently until the vegetables are almost tender. Next add the spinach or cabbage, and cook for a further 5 minutes, until softened. Season with salt and freshly ground black pepper; cook for a further 2–3 minutes.

Fluff the rice by stirring gently with a fork, then serve with the spiced vegetables.

Paella ⊻ ♀

This is a very pretty and tasty dish. Don't be put off by the number of ingredients — it's easy to make and only needs a green salad, or a lettuce, onion and tomato salad, to go with it. If there's any over, it's very good served cold, as a salad.

Serves 3–4

2 tablespoons olive oil
1 large onion, peeled and chopped
6 celery sticks, trimmed and cut into 5 mm/¼ inch dice
1 garlic clove, peeled and crushed
½ teaspoon turmeric powder
1 teaspoon dried basil
100 g (4 oz) brown rice
300 ml (10 fl oz) water
salt and freshly ground black pepper
1 small red pepper, de-seeded and sliced
1 small yellow pepper, de-seeded and sliced
1 small green pepper, de-seeded and sliced
100 g (4 oz) green beans, trimmed and cut into 2 cm/1 inch
   lengths
50 g (2 oz) black olives
2 tablespoons chopped fresh parsley

Heat the oil in a large saucepan and fry the onion for 5 minutes, stirring often. Then add the celery, cover and fry for a further 5 minutes, stirring from time to time. Add the garlic, turmeric, basil, rice and water. Season with salt and pepper, then bring to the boil. Cover, turn down the heat, and leave to simmer over the lowest possible heat for 30 minutes.

Then open the lid and add all the vegetables, but don't mix them in. Turn the heat up slightly, cover and leave for a further 15 minutes, or until the vegetables are just tender. Gently mix the vegetables into the rice, add the olives and chopped parsley, check the seasoning, turn into a large, warmed shallow dish, and serve.

✳

Rice with Courgettes Ⓥ

A light, summery dish to make when there are plenty of courgettes, tomatoes and peppers. It's nice served with a salad of crisp summer lettuce and chopped mint.

Serves 4

700 g (1½ lb) courgettes
salt
40 g (½ oz) butter or 3 tablespoons olive oil
1 large onion, peeled and finely chopped
700 g (1½ lb) tomatoes, skinned and roughly chopped
1 large garlic clove, peeled and crushed
1 rounded tablespoon tomato purée
freshly ground black pepper
1 large red pepper, de-seeded and chopped
175 g (6 oz) brown rice
1–2 tablespoons chopped parsley

Start by washing the courgettes and trimming the ends. Then cut them into slices 5 mm/¼ inch thick, sprinkle with salt and place in a colander. Leave for 1 hour, to remove excess water, then rinse, drain well and pat dry with kitchen paper.

While this is happening, melt the butter or oil in a large saucepan, add the onion, cover and fry gently for 5 minutes, stirring often. Then add the tomatoes, garlic, tomato purée and a seasoning of salt and pepper. Mix well, then cover and simmer gently for 15 minutes, stirring often. Add the courgettes and pepper, cover and simmer for a further 10 minutes, then put in the rice and stir well. Cover once again, and leave over a gentle heat, stirring occasionally, until the rice is tender: about 40 minutes. Check the seasoning, sprinkle with chopped parsley and serve.

Risotto ◐

This is nicest when made with Italian Arborio rice (which you can get from Italian shops and from Sainsbury's). A susbsitute would be round-grain or pudding rice, which is easy to get anywhere. Serve the risotto with a tomato salad or a green salad.

Serves 3

50 g (2 oz) butter
1 onion, peeled and chopped
1 garlic clove, peeled and crushed
300 g (10 oz) Arborio rice or pudding rice
1 litre (1¾ pints) boiling water
salt and freshly ground black pepper
4 tablespoons Parmesan cheese, grated
1–2 tablespoons chopped parsley
extra grated Parmesan cheese to serve

Melt half the butter in a large saucepan, then add the onion and fry gently, with a lid on the pan, for 5 minutes. Stir in the garlic and rice, and fry for a further 2–3 minutes, stirring all the time, then add 300 ml (½ pint) of the boiling water and stir. Cook gently, uncovered, stirring often, until the water has been absorbed by the rice. Then add another 300 ml (½ pint) water and continue in this way until all the rice is tender and the water has been absorbed. This will take 20–30 minutes. Season, then stir in the remaining butter and the 4 tablespoons Parmesan cheese; serve sprinkled with the chopped parsley. Hand round the extra cheese separately.

Mushrooms in Cream Sauce with Brown Rice ◑ ♀

This is easy to make, yet rich and rather special. Serve with a green salad (page 113) or a mixed lettuce salad.

Serves 4

225 g (8 oz) long grain brown rice
700 g (1½ lb) button mushrooms
50 g (2 oz) butter
2 large garlic cloves, peeled and chopped
2 tablespoons brandy
300 ml (10 fl oz) double cream
freshly grated nutmeg
salt and freshly ground black pepper

Bring a large saucepan of water to the boil then add a teaspoonful of salt and the rice. Boil, uncovered, for 30 minutes, or until a grain feels tender when you crush it.

While the rice is cooking, prepare the mushroom mixture. Wash the mushrooms quickly and dry them on kitchen paper. Cut any larger mushrooms into halves or quarters, so that they are all about the same size.

Melt the butter in a large saucepan and put in the mushrooms. Fry, stirring often, for 4–5 minutes, until just tender. If the mushrooms make much liquid, turn the heat up and boil until all the liquid has gone. Add the garlic and brandy, stir over the heat for a moment or two, then add the cream and cook gently for a few minutes until thickened. Grate in some nutmeg to taste — about a quarter of a nutmeg — then season with salt and pepper.

Drain the rice, check the seasoning, then serve on a large, warmed serving dish, or on individual plates; make a well in the centre and pour the mushroom mixture into this.

PASTA

Pasta can be made into some excellent vegetarian dishes and is quick and easy to prepare.

The type of pasta most widely available is the ordinary dried sort, white or wholewheat, or perhaps coloured green with spinach or red with tomato. But fresh pasta, which will keep for a day or two in the fridge, can be bought in speciality shops, delicatessens and some supermarkets. The basic cooking is the same for all types, it's just the time which varies.

The first essential for cooking pasta is a really large saucepan, so that the pasta pieces have room to move around without sticking together.

To cook pasta, fill the saucepan almost to the top with water and bring to the boil. Put in the pasta, give it a quick swirl with a spoon, add a teaspoonful of olive oil if you like to help keep the pieces of pasta separate, and bring it quickly up to the boil again. Then let it boil, uncovered, until the pasta is just done. Try a bit — it should still have some 'bite' to it. The time given on the packet will be a guide, but I find it often takes less time than the instructions say, so try some before the time is up. Once the pasta is cooked, drain it; the easiest way to do this is to tip it into a metal colander in the sink. Then put it back into the still-hot saucepan. Add a knob of butter or a tablespoon of olive oil and some salt and freshly ground black pepper, then serve immediately.

Some people put salt into the cooking water before adding the pasta, but I generally add salt after cooking. This is just a personal preference: you can do either.

Fettucine with Cream and Blue Cheese ◑ ♀

A wonderful, quick supper dish. It's rich, so is best served with a simple green salad. The ingredients can be doubled to make enough for four people.

Serves 2

225–350 g (8–12 oz) fettucine or tagliatelle
1 teaspoon olive oil
¼ oz butter
salt and freshly ground black pepper
50 g (2 oz) walnuts, roughly chopped

For the sauce

150 ml (5 fl oz) double cream
1 small garlic clove, peeled and crushed
50 g (2 oz) blue cheese — Danish blue, Stilton or, best of all, Gorgonzola, crumbled

Bring a large saucepanful of water to the boil, add a teaspoonful of salt and of olive oil, then put in the pasta. Give it a quick stir, then bring it back to the boil and cook for 8–10 minutes, or until the pasta is just done.

Meanwhile, make the sauce. Put the cream into a small, heavy-based pan with the garlic and blue cheese. Heat gently for 3–4 minutes, until the cheese has melted, stirring from time to time. When the pasta is ready, drain it thoroughly, then return it to the still-warm saucepan with the butter, some salt and pepper, and the walnuts. Mix lightly with a fork until the butter has melted, then serve the pasta on warmed plates and pour the sauce on top.

Rigatoni with Tomato Sauce ◑

Rigatoni, the big, ribbed pasta, is particularly good in this recipe, because the sauce clings to it well. But spaghetti is also good, in which case you have the classic Spaghetti Napoletana. This is particularly good made with fresh tomatoes but, for speed and economy, canned tomatoes are also very good. If you first put the water on to boil, then make the sauce, the pasta and the sauce should be done at the same time, making this an excellent quick meal.

Serves 2

225–350 g (8–12 oz) rigatoni
1 teaspoon olive oil
salt and freshly ground black pepper
8 g (¼ oz) butter

For the sauce

450 g (1 lb) tomatoes, or 425 g (15 oz) can tomatoes
1 tablespoon olive oil
1 onion, peeled and chopped
1 teaspoon dried basil
1 large garlic clove, peeled and crushed
salt and freshly ground black pepper
grated Parmesan cheese to serve

Bring a large panful of water to the boil, add a teaspoonful each of salt and olive oil, and add the pasta. Stir, then let the pasta boil, uncovered, for 8–10 minutes, or until just tender.

Meanwhile, peel the tomatoes; put them in a bowl, covering with boiling water and leave for 1–2 minutes, until the skin will slip off easily with the aid of a pointed knife. Then drain them at once, and peel them all. Chop the tomatoes roughly. Alternatively, if you're using canned tomatoes, chop these.

Next, heat the oil in a medium-sized saucepan and fry the onion for 5 minutes with a lid on the pan. Add the tomatoes, basil and the garlic, mix well, then put a lid on the pan and simmer for 15–20 minutes. Season with salt and pepper.

Drain the pasta, return it to the saucepan with the butter and some salt and pepper and stir it with a fork until the butter has melted. Then serve it on warmed dishes and pour the sauce on top. Hand round grated Parmesan cheese separately.

[✳] The sauce freezes well.

Spaghetti with Vegetarian Bolognese Sauce ◐ Ⓥ

The rich mushroom sauce makes an excellent vegetarian alternative to a bolognese sauce. Serve this with a green salad or a mixed salad of lettuce, tomato, and cucumber, pepper or grated carrot.

Serves 2

225–350 g (8–12 oz) spaghetti
1 teaspoon olive oil
8 g (¼ oz) butter or 2 teaspoons olive oil
salt and freshly ground black pepper

For the sauce

2 tablespoons olive oil
1 onion, very finely chopped
300 g (10 oz) mushrooms
1 large garlic clove, peeled and crushed
225 g (8 oz) can tomatoes
2 tablespoons sherry or 3–4 tablespoons red wine
2 heaped tablespoons tomato purée
1 teaspoon dried basil
1 teaspoon black olive pâté or stoned and mashed black olives
salt and freshly ground black pepper
grated Parmesan cheese to serve (optional)

First make the sauce: heat the oil in a medium-sized saucepan and fry the onion for 5 minutes with a lid on the pan. Meanwhile wipe the mushrooms with a clean damp cloth, then chop them up as finely as possible — they can be done in a food processor, but take care not to purée them completely. Add the mushroom to the onion with the garlic (if you're chopping the mushrooms in a food processor, the whole peeled garlic clove can be peeled and crushed by putting it in with them) and fry for a further 5 minutes, browning lightly and stirring often. Then add the tomatoes, wine, tomato purée, olives and basil. Mix well, then put a lid on the pan and leave the sauce to simmer for 25–30 minutes, until thick.

While the sauce is cooking, bring a large saucepanful of water to the boil and add a teaspoonful of salt and one of olive oil. Hold the spaghetti upright in your hand like a bunch of flowers, and stand it up in the boiling water. As the spaghetti softens, push it down into the water. Give it a quick stir, then leave it to boil for 8–10 minutes, until just tender. Drain thoroughly, then put the spaghetti back into the saucepan with the butter or oil and a seasoning of salt and pepper. Serve the spaghetti on a hot serving dish or individual plates and top with the sauce. Hand round grated Parmesan cheese separately, if wanted.

⊠ The sauce freezes well.

Creamy Macaroni Bake ◑

This is a bit like macaroni cheese. It can be finished under the grill or in the oven. Serve it with a tomato salad.

Serves 4

225 g (8 oz) quick-cook or wholewheat macaroni
65 g (2½ oz) butter
50 g (2 oz) flour
700 ml (1¼ pints) water
3-4 tablespoons double cream
2 teaspoons made mustard, preferably Dijon
salt and freshly ground black pepper
dried wholewheat breadcrumbs for topping
shallow flameproof dish, well-buttered (one which will fit under the grill if you're using this cooking method)

Heat the grill or preheat the oven to 200°C/400°F/Gas Mark 6.

Bring a large saucepanful of water to the boil, put in the macaroni and cook, uncovered, for 8–10 minutes, or until the macaroni is just tender. Then drain the macaroni. Meanwhile, make the sauce. Melt 50 g (2 oz) of the butter in a saucepan and add the flour. After a moment or two, add the water in three batches, stirring well after each. Let the mixture simmer for 10 minutes, then remove from the heat and add the cream, mustard and seasoning. Mix well, then turn the mixture into the prepared dish and sprinkle the breadcrumbs on top. Cut the remaining butter into small pieces and scatter these over the top of the breadcrumbs.

Place the dish under the preheated grill for about 10 minutes, to heat through and crisp the top; or bake in the oven for 20–30 minutes, until the macaroni cheese is hot inside and brown and crisp on top.

Vegetarian Lasagne al Forno ♀

This is a very good vegetarian lasagne. It does take a bit of time to make, but it can be made well in advance, ready for baking later, and is an excellent way of feeding a crowd.

Serves 4-6

225–350 g (8–12 oz) lasagne verde
1 teaspoon salt
1 teaspoon olive oil
freshly grated Parmesan cheese

For the mushroom sauce

2 tablespoons olive oil
1 onion, very finely chopped
300 g (10 oz) mushrooms
1 large garlic clove, peeled and crushed
225 g (8 oz) can tomatoes
2 tablespoons sherry or 3–4 tablespoons red wine
2 heaped tablespoons tomato purée
1 teaspoon dried basil
1 teaspoon black olive pâté or stoned and mashed black olives
salt and freshly ground black pepper

For the cream sauce

50 g (2 oz) butter
50 g (2 oz) plain flour
900 ml (1½ pints) milk
150 ml (¼ pint) single cream
freshly grated nutmeg
salt and freshly ground black pepper
shallow casserole dish or roasting tin 19 × 29 cm/7½ × 11½ inches

First make the mushroom mixture. Heat the oil in a medium-sized saucepan and fry the onion for 5 minutes with a lid on the pan. Meanwhile wipe the mushrooms with a clean damp cloth, then chop them up as finely as possible — they can be done in a food processor, but take care not to purée them completely (the garlic may be crushed with them). Add the mushrooms to the onion with the garlic and fry for a further 5 minutes, browning lightly and stirring often. Then add the tomatoes, wine, tomato purée, basil and black olives. Mix well, then put a lid on the pan and leave the sauce to simmer for 25–30 minutes, until thick.

Meanwhile, make the cream sauce. Melt the butter in a medium saucepan, then add the flour. Stir over the heat for a moment, then add a third of the milk. Stir until thick, then stir in another third and stir again. Repeat with the final third, stirring until the sauce is smooth. Leave the sauce to cook over a very gentle heat for 10 minutes, then remove from the heat and stir in the cream, a good grating of nutmeg and salt and pepper to taste.

While the sauce is cooking, unless you are using oven-ready lasagne, which can be used dry, bring a large saucepanful of water to the boil and add a teaspoonful of salt and one of olive oil. Put in the lasagne and cook for about 8 minutes (2–3 minutes for fresh lasagne). Drain the lasagne and place in a bowl of cold water to prevent the sheets from sticking together.

To assemble the lasagne, first grease the dish thoroughly, then arrange sheets of lasagne in the base, to cover it. On top of this put first a layer of half the mushroom sauce, then one of cream sauce, using a third of the sauce. Top this with another layer of lasagne, then the rest of the mushroom sauce followed by half the remaining cream sauce. Finish with a layer of lasagne followed by the remainder of the cream sauce. Sprinkle with grated Parmesan. The dish can now wait until you're ready to bake it, when it needs to go into a moderate oven, 180°C/350°F/Gas Mark 4, for about 35 minutes.

[✳] Before baking.

VEGETABLE DISHES

A substantial vegetable dish can be made into the main dish of the meal, served with another contrasting vegetable or a salad, perhaps, or with potatoes or rice.

Some of these vegetable main dishes do not contain extra protein ingredients, but having an all-vegetable meal sometimes is healthy and delicious.

You can, however, always add protein ingredients if you like: roasted almonds or cashew nuts, drained red kidney, cannellini or butter beans, or grated cheese, can be served, as I've suggested in some of the recipes.

Or you could serve a protein-rich first course, such as Hummus (page 27) or Lentil Soup (page 23) or finish the meal with biscuits and cheese or yogurt.

Stir-Fried Vegetables Ⓥ ♀

This is a pretty mixture of vegetables which, with some mashed potatoes or boiled brown rice, makes a delicious meal. Don't let the long list of ingredients put you off; it's really very simple! Once the vegetables have been prepared — and this can be done in advance — the dish can be speedily cooked. It's a recipe that I've adapted from *The Dinner Party Book*, by Alexandra Carlier, published by Collins.

Serves 4

450 g (1 lb) broccoli
225 g (8 oz) mangetout, topped and tailed
1 leek, washed and trimmed
several parsley stalks (optional)
a few sprigs of thyme (optional)
75 ml (3 fl oz) olive oil
75 ml (3 fl oz) water
rind from 1 lemon, cut off thinly without any of the
    white pith
10 medium carrots, peeled or scraped and cut lengthwise into
    quarters
450 g (1 lb) button mushrooms, washed quickly and dried
    on kitchen paper, then larger ones halved or quartered
4 large red peppers, cored, de-seeded and cut into strips
2 bunches of spring onions, topped, tailed and trimmed
6 large garlic cloves, peeled and crushed or finely chopped
salt and freshly ground black pepper
2 tablespoons chopped parsley

Bring a large saucepanful of water to the boil. Meanwhile, wash the broccoli thoroughly, then divide it into florets and cut the stalks off. Cut off any tough, knobbled part from the broccoli stalks, then cut the stalks into pieces the size of matchsticks. Add the broccoli matchsticks to the saucepan of boiling water and boil for 3–4 minutes, then add the broccoli florets and boil for 1 minute longer. Quickly remove all the broccoli with a perforated spoon and place it in a colander. Place under a cold running tap to cool the broccoli quickly, then drain thoroughly and leave on one side.

Bring the pan of water back to the boil, then add the mangetout and boil for 1 minute. Drain and cool under cold running water, as for the broccoli. Drain again, and leave on one side.

Make a slit in the side of the leek without cutting it right in half, then push the parsley stalks and thyme sprigs, if you're using these, into the leek and tie up with some string to keep them in place. Put this leek bouquet garni into a saucepan large enough to hold all the vegetables — I use my pressure cooker pan. Add the oil, water and lemon peel and bring to the boil, then put in the carrots, half cover, and simmer for 4 minutes.

After this, remove from the heat and leave on one side until you want to complete the dish.

About 5 minutes before you want to eat, bring the carrot mixture back to the boil, then add all the remaining vegetables and the garlic. Cook over a high heat, stirring frequently, for about 5 minutes, until all the vegetables are just tender. Season with salt and pepper. This is attractive served from a large, shallow casserole dish, previously warmed. Sprinkle the parsley on top just before serving.

Potato Bake

This dish is quick and easy to make but you need to allow a good hour for it to cook, and it will not spoil if it's left in the oven for longer. Some cheese can be included in the layers (grated Cheddar-type, or, better but more expensive, thinly-sliced Gruyère), although I personally prefer this simpler version, with a green salad or a tomato salad, and some soured cream and herb sauce (page 138) to accompany it. If you're using cheese, you'll need about 175 g (6 oz), and the butter can be reduced to 15 g (½ oz).

Serves 3

50 g (2 oz) butter
900 g (2 lb) potatoes, peeled and cut into thin slices — no thicker than 5 mm/¼ inch
1 onion, peeled and very thinly sliced
salt and freshly ground black pepper
freshly grated nutmeg
4 tablespoons single cream
shallow ovenproof dish

Preheat the oven to 180°C/350°F/Gas Mark 4. Melt the butter and use some of it to grease a shallow ovenproof dish.

Arrange a layer of potato slices in the base of the dish, put some of the onion rings on top and season with salt, pepper and a grating of nutmeg. Repeat these layers, until all the vegetables are used, ending with a layer of potato. Pour the cream and the remaining butter over the top and finish with a final grating of nutmeg. Cover with foil and bake for 1 hour, removing the foil for the last half-hour to brown the top. The bake is done when you can easily push the point of a knife through the potato.

Vegetable Crumble V

Serve this with just a green salad or cooked green vegetable to accompany, and some creamy mashed potatoes, too, for a more substantial meal.

Serves 4

2 tablespoons olive oil
1 large onion, peeled and chopped
2 carrots, scraped and cut into 5 mm/¼ inch dice
225 g (8 oz) courgettes, trimmed and cut into 5 mm/¼ inch dice
425 g (15 oz) can tomatoes, chopped
100 g (4 oz) button mushrooms, quickly washed, dried and sliced
salt and freshly ground black pepper

For the crumble

175 g (6 oz) plain wholewheat flour
pinch of salt
75 g (3 oz) butter or margarine
2 teaspoons dried mixed herbs
shallow ovenproof casserole dish, lightly greased

Preheat the oven to 200°C/400°F/Gas Mark 6.

Make the vegetable mixture. Heat the oil in the saucepan and add the onion and carrot; stir, then cover and fry gently for 10 minutes. Add the courgettes, tomatoes and mushrooms, stir well, cover and cook for a further 10–15 minutes, or until the vegetables are tender. Season the mixture with salt and pepper.

Meanwhile make the crumble topping. Put the flour into a bowl with the salt. Cut the butter into rough pieces, then add them to the bowl and rub them into the flour with your finger tips, until the mixture looks like breadcrumbs. Add the herbs and mix well.

Put the vegetable mixture into the casserole dish then pour the crumble on top in an even layer. Bake for 30 minutes, until the crumble is crisp and lightly browned.

VARIATION

Vegetable and Hazel Nut Crumble

Make this exactly as described above, but add 100 g (4 oz) coarsely-ground hazel nuts (the skinned kind) to the crumble mixture after you've rubbed the fat into the flour.

Aubergine Bake

This dish is a little more time-consuming to make than some, although all the work can be done in advance, ready for baking later. It's rich and delicious, good for informal entertaining: serve with red wine and a crunchy bitter-leaf green salad with a good dressing (page 113).

Serves 4

800 g (1½ lb) aubergines
salt
6 rounded tablespoons plain wholewheat flour
about 120 ml (4 fl oz) olive oil for shallow frying
350 g (12 oz) Mozzarella cheese, thinly sliced
25 g (1 oz) Parmesan cheese, grated

For the sauce

1 tablespoon olive oil
1 onion, peeled and chopped
1 large garlic clove, peeled and crushed
425 g (15 oz) can tomatoes
1 teaspoon dried basil
4 tablespoons red wine
salt and freshly ground black pepper
shallow ovenproof dish

First of all wipe the aubergines and cut off the stalks; do this carefully, as it's easy to get tiny splinters in your hands. Then cut the aubergines into rounds 5 mm/¼ inch wide. Put these into a colander, sprinkling with salt between the layers. Place a plate and a weight on top, and leave on the draining board for 30 minutes, to extract any bitter juices, and to make the aubergines less absorbent, so that when you fry them they won't take up so much oil.

Meanwhile, make the sauce. Heat the oil in a medium-sized saucepan and fry the onion for 5 minutes with a lid on the pan. Add the garlic, tomatoes, basil and wine. Mix well, chopping the tomatoes a bit with the spoon, then put a lid on the pan and simmer for 15–20 minutes. Season with salt and pepper.

Now rinse the aubergines under cold running water, then squeeze them to extract as much liquid as possible. Toss the aubergines in the flour. Heat 3 mm/⅛ inch olive oil in a frying pan, then fry the aubergine slices in batches, turning them over to brown both sides. Lift them out and drain them on crumpled kitchen paper. Add more oil to the frying pan as necessary.

Put a layer of aubergine slices in the base of the shallow ovenproof dish and cover with a layer of cheese slices. Continue in this way until all the aubergine and cheese has been used, ending with cheese. Pour the tomato sauce over the top, then sprinkle with the Parmesan.

Bake at 200°C/400°F/Gas Mark 6 for about 20 minutes, or until the cheese is bubbling.

✱ Before baking.

Stuffed Aubergines ♀

This is another special-occasion dish which can be fully prepared beforehand, ready for baking later. The initial baking of the whole aubergines can be done at a convenient time when the oven is on for something else, to save time and heat. Serve these aubergines with buttered brown rice, or creamy mashed potatoes or new potatoes and a crisp green salad.

Serves 4

2 medium-sized aubergines
3 tablespoons olive oil
1 large onion, peeled and chopped
425 g (15 oz) can tomatoes
1 teaspoon dried basil
1 garlic clove, peeled and crushed
salt and freshly ground black pepper
175 g (6 oz) button mushrooms, washed quickly, dried and
    sliced
100 g (4 oz) cottage cheese
1 tablespoon chopped fresh parsley
50 g (2 oz) Parmesan cheese, grated
*shallow ovenproof dish big enough to hold the aubergines,
    greased*

Set the oven to 200°C/400°C/Gas Mark 6.
   Cut the stalk ends of the aubergines, handling them carefully to avoid getting splinters in your fingers. Then score the aubergines lengthwise with a sharp knife — as if you were cutting them in half lengthwise, but just cutting the skin. Place the aubergines on a dry baking sheet and bake for about 30 minutes, or until they feel tender when pierced with a knife.
   While the aubergines are cooking, make a simple tomato sauce. Heat 2 tablespoons of the oil in a medium-sized saucepan and fry the onion for 5 minutes with a lid on the pan. Add the tomatoes, basil and the garlic, mix well, then

put a lid on the pan and simmer for 15–20 minutes. Season with salt and pepper.

When the aubergines are ready, let them cool slightly, then cut them in half through the original score marks. Scoop the flesh out of the skins and into a bowl with a teaspoon, being careful not to break the skins. Put the skins into a lightly-greased shallow ovenproof dish.

Fry the mushrooms in the remaining tablespoon of oil for about 4 minutes, until just tender, then add the aubergine mixture in the bowl, together with 2 tablespoons of the tomato sauce, the cottage cheese, parsley and half the grated Parmesan. Season with salt and freshly ground black pepper. Spoon this mixture into the aubergine skins, sprinkle with the remaining Parmesan cheese. Pour the rest of the tomato sauce into the casserole around the aubergine skins and bake at 190°C/375°F/Gas Mark 5 for about 30 minutes, or until golden brown.

Stuffed Peppers ⊻ ♀

This is another dish which is suitable for a special occasion, and it can be prepared in advance, ready for baking later. Choose peppers with a good squarish shape, so that they will hold the stuffing mixture well.

Serves 4

100 g (4 oz) brown rice
4 medium-sized green, red, yellow or black peppers, or a mixture
2 tablespoons olive oil
1 large onion, peeled and chopped
1 teaspoon dried thyme
2 large tomatoes, skinned and chopped, or 225 g (8 oz) can tomatoes, chopped
50 g (2 oz) chopped walnuts
2 heaped tablespoons chopped fresh parsley
salt and freshly ground black pepper
50 g (2 oz) grated cheese (optional)
shallow ovenproof dish big enough to hold the peppers, greased

Half fill a medium to large saucepan with water, bring to the boil, then put in the rice and boil, half-covered, for 30 minutes, or until just tender, then drain.

Cut a small slice off the stalk end of the peppers, then scoop out the seeds and rinse under the cold tap. Bring a large saucepanful of water to the boil and put in the peppers and the sliced-off tops. Simmer for 4 minutes, then drain and refresh under cold water. Drain again and pat dry on kitchen paper.

Heat the oil in a saucepan and add the onion. Fry, with a lid on the pan, for 10 minutes, then remove from the heat and add the rice, thyme, tomatoes, walnuts, parsley and seasoning to taste. Stand the peppers in a shallow greased ovenproof dish. Spoon the rice mixture into the peppers; top with the grated cheese, unless a vegan dish is required.

Bake at 200°C/400°F/Gas Mark 6 for 30 minutes, until the cheese has melted and lightly browned. Serve with light, creamy mashed potatoes or puréed carrots and a green salad.

Vegetable Casserole [V]

This is a simple yet delicious mixture of vegetables. Many different types can be used, varying the flavours and textures as much as possible, and the casserole can either be cooked on top of the stove or in the oven, whichever is most convenient. It's delicious served with brown rice, baked potatoes or mashed potatoes.

Serves 4
2 tablespoons olive oil
1 onion, peeled and chopped
2 leeks, trimmed, washed and sliced
2 medium-large carrots, scraped and diced
1–2 medium parsnips, peeled and diced
1 fennel bulb, sliced
1 small green or red pepper, de-seeded and sliced
2 sticks of celery, sliced
1 garlic clove, peeled and crushed
425 g (15 oz) can tomatoes
4 large, flat mushrooms, quartered, or 225 g (8 oz) button
   mushrooms
425 g (12 oz) red kidney beans, drained
salt and freshly ground black pepper

Set the oven to 150°C/300°F/Gas Mark 1 if you're going to use this cooking method. Then heat 1 tablespoonful of the oil in a large saucepan and fry the onion for 5 minutes. Add the leeks, carrots, parsnips, fennel, pepper and celery, stir well, then cover and cook very gently for 10 minutes, stirring from time to time. Next add the garlic and tomatoes. If you're using the oven, transfer the mixture to a casserole, cover, and cook for about 1 hour, or until the vegetables are tender. To cook the casserole on top of the stove, cover the saucepan and cook over a low heat for 20–30 minutes, until all the vegetables are tender. Just before the vegetables are ready, fry the mushrooms quickly in the remaining oil for 4–5 minutes until just tender. Add the mushrooms to the casserole together with the red kidney beans, mix well, and add seasoning to taste. Let the casserole cook for a further 10 minutes to heat through the beans, then serve.

NUT DISHES

Nuts can be made into some very tasty and nutritious savouries. Once someone has tasted a good nut loaf or burgers they stop joking — and ask for the recipe!

Although nuts are expensive to buy, they are concentrated, and it only takes 100–200 g (4–8 oz) to make a filling main course to feed 4–6 people.

Buy nuts in small quantities from a shop with a rapid turnover and use them up quickly. They can be ground, if required, by whizzing them in a liquidizer, food processor or electric coffee mill, or with a little hand grinder which can be bought quite cheaply. Or, for speed, ground almonds, or mixed chopped nuts, can be used.

Some nuts are improved by roasting them before use. This is particularly true of hazel nuts. The pale golden brown ones which you can buy have already been skinned and lightly roasted. If you buy dark brown unskinned hazel nuts, spread them out on a dry baking sheet and bake at 190°C/375°F/ Gas Mark 5 for about 20 minutes, or until the skins will rub off easily and the nuts underneath are golden brown. Leave the nuts to cool, then rub the skins off with a soft cloth.

Other nuts can be roasted as above, but almonds need to be blanched first, as the skins won't loosen in the same way.

To blanch almonds, put them into a small saucepan, cover with cold water and bring to the boil. Boil for 1 minute, then remove from the heat, drain and slip the skins off with your fingers.

Savoury Mushroom, Nut and Tomato Bake [V]

Serve this savoury bake with a vegetarian gravy (p 135) and some cooked vegetables, such as sprouts or broccoli and new potatoes. If there's any over, it makes an excellent filling for green peppers — prepare these as described on page 71.

Serves 4

100 ml (4 fl oz) vegetable oil
225 g (8 oz) soft wholewheat breadcrumbs (see page 200)
100 g (4 oz) mixed grated nuts, any types
1 small onion, peeled and finely grated
225 g (8 oz) button mushrooms, quickly washed, dried and
   sliced
225 g (8 oz) tomatoes, skinned and chopped, or 225 g
   (8 oz) can tomatoes, chopped
1 teaspoon dried basil
salt and freshly ground black pepper
deep casserole dish, lightly greased

Set the oven to 190°C/375°F/Gas Mark 5.
   Heat 75 ml (3 fl oz) of the oil in a large frying pan and fry the breadcrumbs, nuts and onion for about 5 minutes, until browned and crisp, stirring frequently. Remove from the frying pan, put in the rest of the oil and fry the mushrooms for 4–5 minutes. Remove from the heat and add the tomatoes. Add the basil and season with salt and pepper.
   Put a layer of the crumb mixture in the bottom of the casserole then spoon some of the mushroom and tomato mixture on top, followed by more of the crumb mixture. Continue like this until all the mixture has been used, ending with a crumb layer. Bake for 30 minutes. Serve from the dish.

Nut Roast

This nut roast is moist, tasty and delicious: hot, it can be sliced and served with roast potatoes, cooked vegetables and a vegetarian gravy (page 135) as a roast-meat replacement. Cold, it can be sliced, for serving in sandwiches or with salads.

Serves 6

65 g (2½ oz) butter
2 medium onions, finely chopped
1 teaspoon dried thyme
1 teaspoon dried basil
1 tablespoon plain wholewheat flour
200 ml (7 fl oz) water
1 tablespoon soy sauce
1 tablespoon lemon juice
1 tablespoon tomato purée
1 teaspoon yeast extract
1 large garlic clove, peeled and crushed
225 g (8 oz) mixed nuts, such as cashews, hazel nuts and
  a few walnuts, half ground, half roughly chopped
175 g (6 oz) soft wholewheat breadcrumbs
2 eggs, beaten
salt and freshly ground black pepper
butter for greasing the tin
4 tablespoons dried breadcrumbs
900 g (2 lb) loaf tin

Set the oven to 190°C/375°F/Gas Mark 5. Line a 900 g/ 2 lb loaf tin with a strip of greaseproof or non-stick paper, to cover the base and extend up to the narrow sides of the tin. Grease the tin with butter then sprinkle with half the dried crumbs — this will ensure that the nut roast will turn out of the tin easily, and will also give it a crispy outside.

Heat the butter in a large saucepan and fry the onion for 10 minutes with a lid on the pan. Add the herbs, cook for a few seconds, then stir in the flour. Cook for a moment, then add the water. Cook for 2–3 minutes, until thickened, then stir in the soy sauce, lemon juice, tomato purée, yeast extract and garlic. Remove from the heat and add the remaining ingredients, except the dry crumbs. Mix well and season with salt and pepper. Spoon into the prepared tin and level the top. Sprinkle with the remaining crumbs and dot with butter. Bake, uncovered, for about 1 hour, or until the roast feels firm in the centre. Remove from the oven, but leave the roast in the tin for 5 minutes, then slip a knife round the edges to loosen, turn the nut roast out on to a warmed plate and strip off the paper.

VARIATION

Nut Burgers

For delicious nut burgers, make the mixture exactly as described, but use only about 150 ml (5 fl oz) water, just enough to make a mixture that is firm enough to shape. Form into burgers, coat in flour or dried breadcrumbs or, for a very crisp coating, first dip into beaten egg and then into dried breadcrumbs. Fry on both sides in a little hot fat in a frying pan; drain on kitchen paper.

⊠ Both the Nut Roast and the Burgers freeze well, either before or after cooking.

Stuffed White Nutroast Ⓥ ♀

This makes a large roast, enough to serve 4–6 people twice, once hot and once cold. We like this roast for special occasions, and it goes well with all the traditional Christmas accompaniments — Cranberry Sauce (page 137), Vegetarian Gravy (page 135), Bread Sauce (page 138), as well as roast potatoes and seasonal vegetables.

Serves 8–12

25 g (1 oz) butter or margarine
2 large onions, peeled and finely chopped
2 heaped tablespoons flour
300 ml (10 fl oz) milk or water
225 g (8 oz) cashew nuts, finely grated
125 g (4 oz) soft white breadcrumbs
2 tablespoons lemon juice
salt, pepper and freshly grated nutmeg

For the stuffing

175 g (6 oz) soft white breadcrumbs
75 g (3 oz) butter or margarine
1 small onion, peeled and grated
grated rind of 1 well-scrubbed lemon
1 teaspoon mixed dried herbs
a big handful of fresh parsley, chopped
900g/2 lb loaf tin, well-greased, and lined in the base and up the narrow sides with greased non-stick or greaseproof paper

Set the oven to 190°C/375°F/Gas Mark 5.

Melt the butter or margarine in a large saucepan, then put in the onions and fry them gently, with a lid on the pan, for about 10 minutes, or until tender. Stir occasionally, and don't let them brown. Then add the flour, stir for a moment over the heat, then pour in the milk or water and stir until thickened. Remove from the heat and add the nuts, breadcrumbs, lemon juice and salt, pepper and grated nutmeg. Leave on one side while you make the stuffing.

To make the stuffing, put the breadcrumbs into a bowl

and add the rest of the ingredients, and a little salt and pepper. Mix with a fork until combined, then form into a flat rectangle the size of the loaf tin.

Spoon half the nut mixture into the loaf tin, level the surface, then place the rectangle of stuffing on top. Cover with the remaining nut mixture, smooth with the back of a spoon. Bake for 1 hour, or until firm in the middle and lightly browned on top. Remove from the oven and leave to stand for 4–5 minutes, then slip a knife round the sides to loosen, invert a warm serving plate on top, and turn out the nut roast. Garnish with parsley and lemon.

Hazel Nut and Vegetable Burgers ◐ Ⓥ

These burgers are good served in burger buns, or with salad. For a more substantial meal, serve them with fluffy brown rice, a salad and a yogurt and cucumber dip.

Makes 8

50 g (2 oz) peeled onion
50 g (2 oz) scraped carrot
50 g (2 oz) green pepper de-seeded
several sprigs of parsley
1 garlic clove, peeled
125 g (4 oz) wholewheat bread
200 g (7 oz) hazel nuts, brown skins removed
½ teaspoon dried marjoram
salt and freshly ground black pepper
oil for shallow frying

These are very quick to make if you have a food processor; just cut the vegetables and bread into rough chunks, then put into the food processor with the parsley, whole garlic clove, nuts, marjoram and a little salt and pepper. Whizz until smooth.

If you're making the burgers by hand, chop or grate the vegetables as finely as possible, chop the parsley, crush the garlic, grind the nuts and make the bread into crumbs.

Then mix all the ingredients together, adding a little water if necessary, so that it all holds together. Form the mixture into 8 flat round burgers.

To fry the burgers, cover the base of a frying pan with oil to a depth of about 3 mm/⅛ inch and heat. When it's hot, put in the burgers — if it's hot enough, the fat should sizzle as soon as the burgers are put in, but it's important that the outside does not brown too quickly, before the inside is heated through and cooked. Fry for 2–3 minutes, until the underneath is browned and crisp, then turn the burgers over with a palette knife and fry the other side. Drain the burgers on crumpled kitchen paper.

The uncooked burgers can be frozen — spread them out on a plate or baking sheet and freeze until solid, then pack in a suitable container. They can be fried from frozen, but make sure you fry them slowly enough to thaw and cook the centres by the time the outside is done.

VARIATION

Curried Hazel Nut and Vegetable Burgers

Make exactly as described, but replace the marjoram with 1–2 teaspoons curry powder.

Chestnut Sausages ◐ Ⅴ

These are very easy to make and very tasty. I like to serve them as part of a vegetarian Christmas dinner, but they're good any time of the year!

Serves 4

425 g (15 oz) can unsweetened chestnut purée
125 g (4 oz) soft breadcrumbs
grated rind and juice of 1 lemon
1 teaspoon dried thyme
salt and freshly ground black pepper
flour for coating
oil for shallow frying

Put the chestnut purée into a bowl and mash and beat with a wooden spoon until smooth. Then mix in the breadcrumbs, lemon rind and juice, thyme and some salt and pepper to taste. Mix well, then form golf-ball sized pieces into sausage shapes and coat in flour.

To fry the sausages, cover the base of a frying pan with oil to a depth of about 5 mm/¼ inch and heat. When it's hot, put in one of the sausages — if it's hot enough, the fat should sizzle immediately. If so, put in several more, and fry for about 4 minutes, until the underneath is browned and crisp, then turn each sausage over on to its side with a palette knife and fry, before turning it over again, then finally fry the fourth side, so that you end up with perfectly crisp sausages. Drain the sausages on crumpled kitchen roll.

Spread them out on a tray to freeze, then pack. They can be fried from frozen, but cook them gently so that the inside is done by the time the outside is cooked.

CHEESE AND EGG DISHES

Cheese and eggs are both excellent sources of protein and are particularly quick and easy to use. The most healthy way to eat cheese, eggs (and cream), in my opinion, is as part of a main course in a diet which contains plenty of fresh fruit, vegetables and whole grains. (For more about planning a healthy diet, see page 184-6).

Free-range eggs are becoming more and more widely available; I use them for all recipes, and the measurements are based on size 3 free-range eggs.

It's also getting easier to buy cheese which has been made with non-animal rennet: Cheddar, and some other types, are available. When you are using Parmesan cheese in recipes, try to buy a whole piece if possible and grate it yourself, because the flavour is much better. Although it's very expensive, a little goes a long way, and a piece will keep well in a polythene bag in the fridge. For perfection, try to get Italian Mozzarella cheese, which is kept in water in the shop, and is nicer than the Danish vacuum-packed type.

Spanish Omelette ◑

Serves 2

2 tablespoons olive oil
1 onion, peeled and chopped
1 carrot, scraped and coarsely grated
1 small green pepper, de-seeded and chopped
225 g (8 oz) courgettes, diced
1–2 garlic cloves, peeled and crushed
2 tablespoons chopped fresh parsley
4 eggs, beaten
salt and freshly ground black pepper

Heat the oil in a large non-stick frying pan and fry the onion, carrot and pepper, uncovered, for 5 minutes, then add the courgettes and cook for a further 5 minutes. Heat the grill. Add the garlic, parsley and eggs to the vegetables and season with salt and pepper. Stir gently until the omelette starts to set. When the omelette is set underneath, put it under the grill to set the top, but don't let it get too firm or it will be rubbery. Cut the omelette in half and serve immediately.

Cheese Soufflé ♀

Although it isn't difficult to make, I think that a soufflé has a rather celebratory feel about it. It makes a delightful special meal, served with perfectly cooked vegetables such as buttered new potatoes, broccoli florets, whole baby carrots and perhaps a particularly good green salad with fresh herbs.

Serves 4

50 g (2 oz) butter
50 g (2 oz) plain wholewheat flour
225 ml (8 fl oz) milk
100 g (5 oz) cheese, grated
4 eggs, separated
salt and freshly ground black pepper
butter for greasing dish
2–3 tablespoons dried breadcrumbs for lining dish
1 litre/1³/₄ pint soufflé dish or straight-sided casserole

Preheat the oven to 190°C/375°F/Gas Mark 5. Grease the soufflé dish or straight-sided casserole generously with butter, then sprinkle with the dried breadcrumbs, pressing them into the butter. This will give the soufflé a crisp coating.

Next, melt the butter in a medium saucepan and stir in the flour. Cook for 2–3 minutes without browning, then add the milk and stir over the heat until thickened. Remove from the heat and beat in the cheese. Leave to cool, until you can put your hand against the pan.

Separate the eggs, putting the whites into a clean grease-free bowl, and adding the yolks to the cheese mixture, together with a seasoning of salt and pepper. Make sure the whisk is perfectly clean and free from grease, then whisk the whites until they form stiff peaks. Stir a couple of tablespoons of egg white into the cheese mixture to lighten it. Then put all the rest of the egg white on top of the mixture and, using a metal spoon, carefully lift spoonfuls of the sauce mixture over the egg white to incorporate the egg white without losing its fluffiness. When no more egg white is visible, pour the mixture gently into the prepared dish and bake for 40 minutes, until the soufflé is well puffed up. It's done when a skewer inserted into the centre comes out clean. Serve immediately.

Mushroom Roulade ♀

This is basically a soufflé mixture baked in a shallow tin then turned out, spread with a tasty savoury filling, then rolled up like a swiss roll. It's not as difficult to make as it looks, and it makes a super special-occasion dish, served with some lightly cooked vegetables.

Serves 4–6

75 g (3 oz) butter
75 g (3 oz) flour
600 ml (1 pint) milk
salt and freshly ground black pepper
4 eggs
2 tablespoons Parmesan cheese, grated
parsley sprigs, for garnish

For the mushroom filling

25 g (½ oz) butter
225 g (8 oz) mushrooms, thinly sliced
150 ml (5 fl oz) soured cream
freshly grated nutmeg
25 × 38 cm/10 × 15 inch swiss roll tin, lined with greased greaseproof or non-stick paper, so that the paper extends 5 cm/2 inches all round the tin

Preheat the oven to 160°C/325°F/Gas Mark 3.
    Begin by making the roulade mixture. Melt the butter in a medium saucepan and stir in the flour. Cook for 2–3 minutes without browning, then add a third of the milk and stir over the heat until thickened. Then repeat the process with another third of the milk, and finally pour in the last third and mix

well until smooth. Remove from the heat and add 1 teaspoon of salt and a good grating of pepper. Then leave until the pan is cool enough for you to put your hand against the side.

Next, separate the eggs; put the whites into a clean, greasefree bowl and add the yolks to the sauce.

Whisk the whites until they form stiff peaks. Stir a couple of tablespoons of egg white into the sauce to lighten it. Then put all the rest of the egg white on top of the mixture and, using a metal spoon, carefully lift spoonfuls of the sauce mixture over the egg white, to incorporate the egg white without losing its fluffiness. When no more egg white is visible, pour the mixture gently into the prepared tin, pushing it into the corners and levelling the top with the back of a spoon. Bake for 40 minutes, or until golden brown on top.

While the roulade is cooking, make the filling. Melt the butter in a medium pan, add the mushrooms, and fry for 5 minutes. If the mushrooms make a great deal of liquid, turn up the heat and boil hard until this has disappeared. Then remove the pan from the heat and take out 6–8 slices of mushroom for garnishing. Add the soured cream to the rest, together with some salt, pepper and freshly grated nutmeg to taste.

Just before the roulade is ready, spread a large piece of greaseproof paper on top of a clean tea-towel. Sprinkle the greaseproof paper with the Parmesan cheese. Turn the roulade out onto the greaseproof paper and peel off the backing paper.

Quickly reheat the mushroom mixture sauce to just below boiling point, stirring all the time, then spread it over the roulade and, using the greaseproof paper to help, roll the roulade up from one of the short ends. Lift the roulade onto a serving dish and pop it back into the oven for 5–10 minutes to make it piping hot. Garnish with the reserved mushroom slices and the parsley sprigs and serve.

Cheese Egg Pie

This is an easy, comforting, homely dish. It can be prepared in advance, ready for baking when required and an easy vegetable such as frozen peas goes well with it.

Serves 4

600 ml (1 pint) milk
small piece of peeled onion
1 small carrot, scraped
1 bay leaf
50 g (2 oz) butter
2 rounded tablespoons plain wholewheat flour
50 g (2 oz) cheese, grated
6 hard-boiled eggs, peeled and chopped
pinch of mace
salt and freshly ground black pepper
450 g (1 lb) potatoes, boiled and mashed

First flavour the milk for the sauce by heating it in a saucepan with the onion, carrot and bayleaf. Bring to the boil, then remove from the heat, cover and leave for about 15 minutes to infuse. Strain, and discard the onion, carrot and bayleaf.

If you're going to cook the cheese egg pie straight away, preheat the oven at this point to 180°C/350°F/Gas Mark 4. Lightly grease a shallow casserole dish.

Next, make the sauce. Melt the butter in a medium saucepan and stir in the flour. Cook for 2–3 minutes without browning, then add a third of the milk and stir over the heat until thickened. Then repeat the process with another third of the milk, and finally pour in the last third and mix well until smooth. Remove from the heat and stir in the cheese, eggs and mace. Season with salt and pepper.

Pour the mixture into the casserole, then spoon the mashed potato — which should be soft and creamy — on top. Level the top, then draw the prongs of a fork across to make a ridged effect. Bake for 30 minutes.

Cheese Fondue ◗ ♀

Cheese fondue is very quick and easy to make, good for a spur-of-the moment special meal. Although fondue is usually served from a pan set over a table burner, this isn't essential if you use a heavy-based pan to make it in, and serve it really piping hot.

Serves 4

1 garlic clove, peeled and halved
300 ml (10 fl oz) dry cider
400 g (14 oz) Edam cheese, grated
1 tablespoon cornflour
2 tablespoons kirsch or gin (optional)
2 teaspoons lemon juice
salt and freshly ground black pepper
freshly grated nutmeg

To serve

1–2 French bread sticks, cut into bite-sized pieces and warmed in the oven.

Rub the garlic around the inside of a medium, heavy-based saucepan, then discard. Put all but 4 tablespoons of the cider into the saucepan and bring just to the boil, then add the cheese and stir over a gentle heat until melted.

Put the cornflour into a small bowl and mix to a thin paste with the reserved cider and the kirsch or gin if you're using this. Pour the cornflour paste into the cheese mixture, stirring all the time. Boil for a couple of minutes, still stirring, until slightly thickened. Add the lemon juice and salt, pepper and grated nutmeg to taste.

Stand the fondue pan in the centre of the table, on a fondue burner if you have one, with the warmed bread in bowls or baskets nearby. To eat the fondue, people help themselves, spearing a piece of bread with a fondue fork, then dipping it into the bubbling cheese mixture.

Cheese Fritters

These fritters are very popular, especially with children. They're easy to make if you do them in stages. Serve them with lemon slices, chips or mashed potatoes, parsley sauce and a cooked green vegetable or a salad.

Serves 4–6

600 ml (1 pint) milk
1 small onion, peeled and stuck with 1 clove
1 bay leaf
100 g (4 oz) semolina
100 g (4 oz) Cheddar cheese, grated
1–2 tablespoons chopped fresh parsley
½ teaspoon mustard powder
salt and freshly ground black pepper
1 large egg, beaten with 1 tablespoon water
dried breadcrumbs for coating
oil for shallow frying

Bring the milk, onion and bay leaf to the boil in a large saucepan. Then remove from the heat, cover and leave for 10-15 minutes for the flavours to infuse. After that, remove and discard the onion and bay leaf. Return the milk to the boil, then gradually sprinkle the semolina over the top, stirring all the time. Let the mixture simmer for about 5 minutes, stirring often, to cook the semolina. Then remove from the heat and beat in the cheese, parsley, mustard and a good seasoning of salt and pepper.

Brush a large plate or baking sheet with oil. Turn the semolina mixture out onto this and spread it out so that it is about 1 cm/½ inch deep all over. Smooth the surface, then leave to cool completely. It will get firm as it cools.

Cut the semolina mixture into fingers or triangles. Dip these first in the beaten egg, then in the dried breadcrumbs, to coat completely.

Heat 5mm/¼ inch of oil in a frying pan, and fry the cheese fritters for about 4 minutes on each side, or until crisp and golden brown. Drain well on kitchen paper. Serve with lemon slices.

[✳] Spread out on a tray to freeze, then pack. Use from frozen, frying them gently so that the inside is done by the time the outside is cooked.

Easy Wholewheat Pizza ◗

Serves 4

225 g (8 oz) self-raising wholewheat flour, or half wholewheat and half white
½ teaspoon salt
2 teaspoons baking powder
50 g (2 oz) butter
40 g (½ oz) Cheddar cheese, grated
150 ml (5 fl oz) water
olive oil for greasing

For the topping

2 tablespoons oil
2 onions, peeled and chopped
2 tablespoons tomato purée
1 teaspoon dried oregano
salt and freshly ground black pepper
125 g (4 oz) Cheddar cheese, grated
a few black olives (optional)
30 cm/12 inch pizza dish or a baking sheet, brushed with oil

Set the oven to 220°C/425°F/Gas Mark 8.

Put the flour, salt and baking powder into a bowl and rub in the butter until the mixture looks like breadcrumbs, then stir in the grated cheese and water to make a soft dough. Turn the dough onto a lightly floured surface and knead for 1 minute, then cover and leave while you make the topping.

Heat the oil in a saucepan and fry the onion for 10 minutes, with a lid on the pan, until the onion is soft. Remove from the heat and stir in the tomato purée, oregano and salt and pepper to taste. Roll the dough out into a 30 cm/12 inch circle, and place it on the pizza dish or baking sheet. Spoon the filling on top, spreading it to the edges. Then put the grated cheese on top and the black olives if you're using them, and bake for 20–25 minutes, until puffy and golden brown. Serve immediately.

[*] Before or after baking.

Wholewheat Spinach Crêpes with Cream Cheese Stuffing ♀

A frying pan with an inside base measurement of not more than 18 cm/7 inches is best for making pancakes, or crêpes, because the batter can spread right out to the edges, making a neat shape. This is another dish which can be made in advance and baked or reheated later.

Serves 4

100 g (4 oz) plain wholewheat flour
¼ teaspoon salt
2 eggs
300 ml (10 fl oz) milk
2 tablespoons melted butter
100 g (4 oz) frozen spinach purée, thawed and squeezed dry
freshly ground black pepper
freshly grated nutmeg
a little butter for frying

For the filling

225 g (8 oz) cream cheese
225 g (8 oz) curd cheese
4 tablespoons chopped fresh chives or very finely chopped spring onions
salt and freshly ground black pepper
shallow ovenproof dish, about 19 × 29 cm/7½ × 11 inches, lightly greased

The easiest way to make the pancake batter is with a liquidizer or food processor: just put the flour, salt, eggs, milk, butter and spinach into the goblet and whizz until smooth.

To make the batter by hand, put the flour into a bowl with the salt. Make a well in the middle and crack in the eggs. Add about a third of the milk and mix until thick and smooth, then gradually add the rest of the milk, beating well.

Then mix in the melted butter and spinach and grate in some black pepper and nutmeg. The batter can be made several hours in advance if convenient.

To make the pancakes, put a knob of butter about the size of small walnut into the frying pan and melt over a moderate heat. When it has melted, pour all the excess butter on to a saucer — the frying pan should just be shiny and well-greased. Put the frying pan back on the heat, then put in 2 tablespoons of batter mixture. Swirl and tip the frying pan quickly so that the batter runs to the edges of the pan, then let it cook for 1–2 minutes, until set. Then flip it over, using a palette knife, and cook the other side for a further 30–60 seconds. Lift the pancake out and put it on a plate. Continue to make pancakes in this way, piling them up on top of each other on the plate, until all the batter is used up and you have 12–15 pancakes. If necessary, you can leave the pancakes on one side and fill them when needed.

To make the filling, mix together the cheeses until creamy, then beat in the chives or spring onions and some salt and pepper to taste. Put 2 tablespoons of filling onto each pancake and roll them up neatly. Place the filled pancakes side by side in a greased shallow ovenproof dish.

Reheat the pancakes ready for serving for about 30 minutes in an oven pre-heated to 180°C/350°F/Gas Mark 4.

PASTRY

Pastry dishes are popular with most people and are filling and satisfying. I think that pastry made from 100% wholewheat flour is particularly tasty and I use this for nearly all my baking, although I do sometimes use an 85% wholewheat flour or a half-and-half mixture of 100% wholewheat and white flour if I want to make a particularly thin, crisp case for a quiche.

The type of fat you use is a matter of personal preference. I generally use all butter and sometimes a mixture of half butter and half pure white vegetable fat.

Wholewheat shortcrust pastry is made in exactly the same way as white shortcrust and is described in the individual recipes. However, it is a little more crumbly than white pastry, so, when making a pie or flan, it's easier to handle if you roll the pastry out on a board and then slide it straight from the board to the top of the pie or into the flan tin.

A tin is best for making a flan, because it conducts the heat well and helps to produce a crisp result. I use an ordinary fluted 20 cm/8 inch flan tin with a loose base, so that the flan can be lifted out easily for serving.

Cheese and Tomato Flan ◑

This is a light flan with tender pastry that melts in your mouth. The flan can be prepared quite quickly because it does not have to be baked before being filled.

Serves 4

100 g (4 oz) self-raising 85% wholewheat flour
¼ teaspoon salt
65 g (2½ oz) butter

For the filling

100 g (4 oz) cheese, grated
1 tomato, thinly sliced
1–2 teaspoons chopped fresh basil, or ½ teaspoon dried basil
2 eggs
150 ml (5 fl oz) single cream or milk
salt and freshly ground black pepper
20 cm/8 inch flan tin, lightly greased

Preheat the oven to 190°C/375°F/Gas Mark 5. Put a baking sheet in the oven to heat up.

Put the flour into a bowl with the salt. Cut the butter into pieces, and using your finger tips, rub the butter into the flour to make a mixture which looks like fine breadcrumbs. Gather the mixture together to make a dough. It should hold together well because of the slightly higher than usual proportion of fat, but add a few drops of cold water to help bind it together if necessary.

Roll the pastry out on a lightly floured board and lift it into the flan tin. Press it gently into position, then trim the edges. Put the cheese evenly over the bottom of the flan, then arrange the tomato slices on top and sprinkle with basil.

Whisk the egg with the cream or milk and a little salt and pepper, then pour into the flan case on top of the cheese and tomatoes.

Put the flan in the oven on top of the baking sheet, and bake for 35–40 minutes, or until the pastry is crisp and the filling set and lightly browned. Serve hot or warm.

✳ After cooking.

Mushroom Flan

For this flan, the pastry case is baked and then filled with a simple mixture of mushrooms in cream, so the preparation is quite quick. It can be varied by using other mixtures for the filling: cauliflower cheese for instance, or a packet of frozen vegetables cooked and mixed with a cheese sauce (page 137 for the sauce recipe) also make good fillings.

Serves 4

100 g (4 oz) plain wholewheat flour
¼ teaspoon salt
50 g (2 oz) butter
6 teaspoons cold water
1 egg, beaten

For the filling

450 g (1 lb) button mushrooms
25 g (1 oz) butter
2 teaspoons flour
150 ml (5 fl oz) soured cream
salt and freshly ground black pepper
freshly grated nutmeg
paprika pepper
20 cm/8 inch flan tin, lightly greased

Preheat the oven to 200°C/400°F/Gas Mark 6. Put a baking sheet in the oven to heat up.

Put the flour into a bowl with the salt. Cut the butter into pieces, and using your finger tips, rub the butter into the flour to make a mixture which looks like fine breadcrumbs. Add the water, then press the mixture together to make a dough.

Roll the pastry out on a lightly floured board and lift it into the flan tin. Press it gently into position, then trim the edges. Prick the pastry on the bottom of the flan all over with a fork, then put the flan into the oven on top of the baking sheet. Bake for 15–20 minutes, or until brown and crisp. Remove from the oven, brush the base of the flan case all over generously with beaten egg, making sure that the fork marks are filled with egg, then put it back in the oven for a further 5 minutes, to cook the egg and make a crisp, 'waterproof' base.

While the flan case is cooking, prepare the filling. Wash the mushrooms quickly, then dry them on kitchen paper. Halve or quarter any large ones, so that they are all roughly the same size. Heat the butter in a large saucepan and fry the mushrooms for 5–6 minutes, until tender. Add the flour, then cook gently for 4–5 minutes, to cook the flour. Then add the soured cream, season with salt and freshly ground black pepper, and grate in some nutmeg. Heat gently, without letting the mixture boil.

Spoon the mushroom mixture into the flan case, sprinkle with paprika pepper for a flash of bright colour, and serve immediately, or keep the flan warm in a low oven at 150°C/ 300°F/Gas Mark 2.

Cheese and Onion Roll

This pastry roll has a filling which can be prepared very quickly. It is good served with a vegetarian gravy (page 135) and some cooked vegetables.

Serves 4
225 g (8 oz) plain wholewheat flour
½ teaspoon salt
100 g (4 oz) butter
3 tablespoons cold water

For the filling
3 large onions
175 g (6 oz) Cheddar cheese, grated
salt and freshly ground black pepper

Preheat the oven to 200°C/400°F/Gas Mark 6. Lightly grease a large baking sheet.

To make the filling, peel and slice the onions, then cook them in a little water, with a lid on the pan, for about 10 minutes, until the onions are tender but not mushy. Remove from the heat, drain thoroughly, then add the cheese and salt and pepper to taste. Leave to cool while you make the pastry.

Put the flour into a bowl with the salt. Cut the butter into pieces, and using your finger tips, rub the butter into the flour to make a mixture which looks like fine breadcrumbs. Add the water, then press the mixture together to make a dough.

Roll half the pastry out on a lightly floured board into a rectangle and place this on the baking sheet. Spoon the cheese and onion mixture on top of the pastry, leaving 1 cm/½ inch clear all round the edges. Then roll the rest of the pastry out into another rectangle the same size as the last one and place on top of the onion mixture. Press the edges of the pastry together and crimp them with your fingers or with the prongs of a fork. Prick the top of the roll two or three times with a fork to let the steam out. Then bake for 20–25 minutes, or until brown and crisp.

✳ Before or after cooking.

Spiced Vegetable Pasties [V]

These pasties are delicious for a picnic or lunch box; serve them with some crisp lettuce, tomato and spring onions.

Makes 4

225 g (8 oz) plain wholewheat flour
$\frac{1}{2}$ teaspoon salt
100 g (4 oz) butter or margarine
3 tablespoons cold water
beaten egg or a little milk to glaze, or soya milk for vegans

For the filling

1 onion, peeled and chopped
2 tablespoons olive oil
225 g (8 oz) potato, peeled and cut into 5mm/$\frac{1}{4}$ inch dice
1 tablespoon ground coriander
1 teaspoon ground cumin
400 g (15 oz) can chick peas, drained
salt and freshly ground black pepper

Preheat the oven to 200°C/400°F/Gas Mark 6. Lightly grease a large baking sheet.

First make the filling; fry the onions in the oil for 5 minutes, then add the potato and the coriander and cumin. Stir, then cook gently, with a lid on the pan, for 10–15 minutes, until the potatoes are tender. Stir from time to time. Then remove from the heat and add the chick peas. Season to taste with salt and pepper, then leave to cool while you make the pastry.

Put the flour into a bowl with the salt. Cut the butter or margarine into pieces, and using your finger tips, rub the butter into the flour to make a mixture which looks like fine breadcrumbs. Add the water, then press the mixture together to make a dough.

Divide the pastry into four equal-sized pieces, then, on a lightly floured board, roll each out into a circle 15 cm/6 inches across. Spoon a quarter of the potato mixture into the centre, then fold up two opposite sides of the pastry and press them together in the centre to make a pastie shape. Brush the pasties with beaten egg or milk (or soya milk), make a couple of holes to let the steam out, then place them on a baking sheet and bake in the oven for 20–25 minutes, or until brown and crisp.

[✳] Before or after cooking.

Asparagus Triangles ♀

These triangles are delicious with either cooked vegetables or the Pretty Carrot Salad on page 115; a soured cream and herb sauce (page 138) goes well with them. As an alternative to the wholewheat shortcrust pastry, you could use frozen puff — you'll need 2 × 200 g (7 oz) packets; roll out and cut four squares from each packet.

Makes 4

225 g (8 oz) plain wholewheat flour, or half wholewheat flour
  and half white flour
½ teaspoon salt
125 g (4 oz) butter
3 tablespoons cold water
beaten egg or a little milk to glaze

For the filling

1 onion, peeled and chopped
25 g (1 oz) butter
225 g (8 oz) potato, peeled and cut into 5 mm/¼ inch dice
450 g (1 lb) asparagus or 1 × 225 g (8 oz) packet frozen
  asparagus
2 tablespoons double cream
salt and freshly ground black pepper
freshly grated nutmeg

Preheat the oven to 200°C/400°F/Gas Mark 6. Lightly grease a large baking sheet.

First make the filling; fry the onion in the butter for 5 minutes, then add the potato. Stir, then cook gently, with a lid on the pan, for 10–15 minutes, until the potato is tender. Stir from time to time. Then remove from the heat. Trim and cook the fresh asparagus as described on page 122, or cook the frozen asparagus according to the packet directions.

Drain well, then cut the asparagus into 2.5 cm/1 inch lengths. Add the asparagus to the potato mixture, together with the cream and salt, pepper and freshly grated nutmeg to taste. Leave to cool while you make the pastry.

Put the flour into a bowl with the salt. Cut the butter into pieces, and using your finger tips, rub the butter into the flour to make a mixture which looks like fine breadcrumbs. Add the water, then press the mixture together to make a dough.

Roll the pastry out into a 30 cm/12 inch square, then cut this into four 15 cm/6 inch squares. Spoon a quarter of the asparagus mixture into the centre of each square, then fold up two opposite sides of the pastry and press them together in the centre to make a pastie triangle. Crimp the edges of the triangles with the prongs of a fork, then brush them over with beaten egg or milk and make a couple of holes to let the steam out. Then place them on a baking sheet and bake for 20–25 minutes, or until brown and crisp.

Savoury Pudding

This is a vegetarian version of a traditional steak and kidney pudding and is very tasty. I got the idea for the filling from Paul Southey's recipe in his book *Gourmet Cooking Without Meat*, published by Marshall Cavendish. The pudding is delicious served with creamy mashed potatoes and a crisp green salad.

Serves 4

350 g (12 oz) self-raising wholewheat flour
½ teaspoon salt
175 g (6 oz) vegetarian suet, coarsely grated
cold water to mix

For the filling

50 g (2 oz) onion, peeled and finely diced
100 g (4 oz) parsnip, peeled and diced
100 g (4 oz) celery, washed and chopped
100 g (4 oz) frozen peas
175 g (6 oz) cheese, grated
2 tablespoons flour
½ teaspoon dried marjoram
salt and freshly ground black pepper
4 tablespoons water
1.5 litre/2½–3 pint pudding basin, generously greased with butter

To make the filling, mix all the vegetables together with the cheese, flour, marjoram and salt and pepper to taste. Leave on one side while you make the pastry.

To make the pastry, put the flour into a bowl with the salt and add the suet. Mix the suet lightly with the flour — don't rub it in, like you do for ordinary shortcrust pastry. Then add enough cold water to make a smooth dough which leaves the sides of the bowl clean. Leave the pastry to rest for 5 minutes while you grease a 1.5 litre/ 2½–3 pint pudding basin generously with butter. Have ready a large saucepan, which will hold the basin, or a steamer, for cooking the pudding. (Suet crust pastry needs to be used as soon as it is made, while the raising agent in the self-raising flour is still active.)

On a lightly floured board, roll out three quarters of the pastry quite thickly (about 1 cm/½ inch deep) and ease it into the basin, to line it. Spoon the filling into the basin on top of the pastry, add the cold water, then roll out the remaining quarter into a circle to fit the top, dampen the edges with cold water and place on top, as a lid. Cover with a double layer of greaseproof paper and then a piece of foil, pleated in the middle so that they can expand. Tie with string, then place in the steamer over boiling water or put into the saucepan and pour round it boiling water to come half way up the sides of the bowl. Steam for 3 hours. Keep an eye on the water level and top it up with more boiling water from time to time as necessary.

When the pudding is done, remove the foil and greaseproof paper coverings, slip a palette knife down the sides of the bowl to loosen, then turn the pudding out onto a warmed plate.

Wholewheat Vegetable Pie [V]

This is delicious made with a thick, hearty wholewheat pastry crust, though you could use a 200 g (7 oz) packet of frozen puff pastry instead (using non-animal fat).

Serves 4

225 g (8 oz) wholewheat flour
½ teaspoon salt
100 g (4 oz) butter or white vegetable fat, or a mixture of the two
3 tablespoons cold water

For the filling

2 tablespoons olive oil
1 large onion, peeled and chopped
2 carrots, scraped and cut into 5 mm/¼ inch dice
225 g (8 oz) courgettes, trimmed and cut into
   5 mm/¼ inch dice
425 g (15 oz) can tomatoes, chopped
100 g (4 oz) button mushrooms, quickly washed,
   dried and sliced
salt and freshly ground black pepper
*1 litre/*1¾ pint pie dish

First make the vegetable mixture: heat the oil in a saucepan and add the onion and carrot. Stir, then cover and fry gently for 10 minutes. Add the courgettes, tomatoes and mushrooms, stir well, cover and cook for a further 10–15 minutes, or until the vegetables are tender. Season the mixture with salt and pepper. Put the mixture into the pie dish and leave to get cold.

Preheat the oven to 200°C/400°F/Gas Mark 6.

Next, make the pastry. Put the flour into a bowl with the salt. Cut the butter and/or fat into small pieces, then, using your finger tips, rub the fat into the flour to make a mixture which looks like fine breadcrumbs. Add the water, then press the mixture together to make a dough.

Roll the pastry out quite thickly into the same shape as the pie dish but 2.5 cm/1 inch larger all round. Cut off this 2.5 cm/1 inch strip all round the pastry, dampen the rim of the pie dish and place the pastry strip on top. Dampen the pastry strip, then put the large piece of pastry on top, pressing the edges down firmly to seal. Crimp the edges of the pastry with your fingers or with a fork, then with a knife make little cuts on the edge of the pastry where the join is, so that it looks as if the pastry has risen in flaky layers. Make a couple of steam-holes in the pastry, then bake for 25–30 minutes, or until golden brown.

✳ Before baking.

Gourmet Vegetable Pie

Like the previous recipe, this could be topped with a crust made from a 200 g (7 oz) packet frozen puff pastry rather than home-made pastry.

Serves 4

225 g (8 oz) wholewheat flour
½ teaspoon salt
125 g (4 oz) butter and white vegetable fat mixed
3 tablespoons cold water

For the filling

1 onion, peeled and chopped
25 g (1 oz) butter
350 g (12 oz) potato, peeled and cut into 5 mm/¼ inch dice
125 g (4 oz) button mushrooms, washed and sliced
450 g (1 lb) asparagus or 1 × 225 g (8 oz) packet
   frozen asparagus
425 g (15 oz) can artichoke hearts, drained and quartered
150 ml (5 fl oz) double cream
1 tablespoon chopped parsley
salt and freshly ground black pepper
freshly grated nutmeg
1 litre/1¾ pint pie dish

First make the filling; fry the onion in the butter for 5 minutes, then add the potato. Stir, then cook gently, with a lid on the pan, for 10–15 minutes, stirring from time to time, until the potato is tender. Then add the sliced mushrooms and cook for a further 3–4 minutes. Remove from the heat.

Trim and cook the fresh asparagus as described on page 122, or the frozen asparagus according to the packet directions. Drain well, then cut the asparagus into 2.5 cm/ 1 inch lengths. Add the asparagus to the potato mixture, together with the artichoke hearts, cream and parsley. Season with salt, pepper and freshly grated nutmeg to taste. Put the mixture into the pie dish and leave to cool while you make the pastry.

Preheat the oven to 200°C/400°F/Gas Mark 6.

Next, put the flour into a bowl with the salt. Cut the butter and fat into small pieces, then, using your finger tips, rub the fats into the flour to make a mixture which looks like fine breadcrumbs. Add the water, then press the mixture together to make a dough.

Roll the pastry out quite thickly into the same shape as the pie dish but 2.5 cm/1 inch larger all round. Cut off this 2.5 cm/1 inch strip all round the pastry, dampen the rim of the pie dish and place the pastry strip on top. Dampen the pastry strip, then put the large piece of pastry on top, pressing the edges down firmly to seal. Crimp the edges of the pastry with your fingers or with a fork, then with a knife make little cuts on the edge of the pastry where the join is, so that it looks as if the pastry has risen in flaky layers. Make a couple of steam-holes in the pastry, then bake for 25–30 minutes, or until golden brown.

[*] Before cooking.

5. Salads and Salad Dressings

Salads are quick to make, colourful and healthy. A simple salad makes a very pleasant accompaniment to many cooked dishes and is often easier to prepare than a cooked vegetable.

Many vegetarians also like to have a big salad for one of their main meals of the day; this is certainly an excellent source of vitamins, minerals and enzymes. The salad can be a straightforward mixture of raw vegetables, or it can be a sumptuous mixture, with mouthwatering flavourings and dressings.

Most salads are best prepared just before they are needed, from vegetables which are fresh and crisp from the fridge. Some, however, made from firm, non-fragile ingredients such as bean salads, potato salads and cole slaw improve if left for an hour or longer so that the flavours have time to soak in.

It's important to wash salad ingredients well, because even if they don't look dirty, they may be harbouring residues of chemical sprays. When they've been washed, shake off as much water as possible, and either leave them for a while in a colander, for the surface water to dry off, or blot them gently in a clean cloth, or pop them into a salad spinner. At this point you can put them into the fridge to chill and crisp up until you are ready to make the salad.

SALAD DRESSINGS

Blender Mayonnaise ◑

This is quick to make and keeps for about a week in a covered bowl in the fridge. It won't freeze, so unless I'm going to use quite a lot of mayonnaise during the week, which doesn't happen very often, I generally find it best to keep a jar of Hellman's mayonnaise (which keeps for ages) in the fridge and just take out a spoonful whenever I need it.

Makes about 200 ml (7 fl oz)
2 egg yolks
¼ teaspoon salt
¼ teaspoon mustard powder
2–3 grindings of black pepper
2 teaspoons white wine vinegar
2 teaspoons lemon juice
200 ml (7 fl oz) cold-pressed sunflower oil

Put the egg yolks, seasonings, vinegar and lemon juice into a blender or food processor and blend for 1 minute. Then gradually add the oil, drop by drop, through the top of the goblet. When you have added half the oil and the mixture has thickened, you can add the rest more quickly, in a thin stream.

Vinaigrette ◓ Ⅴ

The secret of a successful vinaigrette dressing is to use good ingredients. If you use virgin olive oil, freshly-squeezed lemon juice or wine vinegar, sea salt and freshly ground black pepper, the dressing is bound to taste good. The quantities of oil and lemon juice or vinegar vary a bit, depending on which chef or expert you are talking to, but the most generally accepted formula is three parts oil to one part lemon juice or vinegar. Add salt, pepper, mustard, crushed garlic and fresh herbs, if available, to taste. You can mix the ingredients together in a liquidizer or food processor, shake them in a jam jar, combine them in a bowl with a fork or a whisk, or put them straight into a salad bowl and stir them with the salad servers before putting in the salad; it doesn't matter — there's no mystique about this! I like to make up a small quantity of dressing freshly each time I'm making a salad, rather than make a large quantity and keep it in a jar in the fridge.

Enough for a salad to serve 4–6
½ teaspoon sea salt
1 teaspoon made mustard, such as a good Dijon (like Poupon Grey)
1 tablespoon lemon juice or wine vinegar (I prefer Orleans red wine vinegar)
freshly ground black pepper
3 tablespoons good quality olive oil, preferably virgin
other flavouring ingredients such as garlic and chopped herbs, as desired

Put the salt into a bowl with the mustard, lemon juice or vinegar and a good grinding of black pepper. Mix, then add the oil, a little at a time and stir or whisk until blended, then add any other flavourings.

VARIATION

Mustard Vinaigrette ◑ Ⓥ

For a tangy mixture with a beautifully thick consistency, almost like mayonnaise, increase the amount of Dijon mustard to 1 tablespoon.

SALADS

Cole Slaw ◑ Ⓥ

A delicious basic salad, lovely served with crunchy-skinned baked jacket potatoes for a light lunch.

Serves 4

350 g (12 oz) white cabbage, finely shredded
100 g (4 oz) carrots, scraped and coarsely grated
4 tablespoons mayonnaise, or 2 tablespoons mayonnaise mixed with 2 tablespoons plain yogurt, soured cream or water, or tofu dressing (page 201) for vegans
salt and freshly ground black pepper

Just put all the ingredients into a bowl and mix together.

Potato Salad ◑ Ⓥ

When you're serving a selection of salads, for a buffet meal, a potato salad makes a pleasant addition; it's also good with a light salad main course. This salad is excellent made with new potatoes (I like to leave them in their skins), but it's also good made with old potatoes. I think the important thing is to cook the potatoes so that they're still slightly firm. This salad is equally good made with either vinaigrette or mayonnaise.

Serves 4

700 g (1½ lb) potatoes, scrubbed or peeled and cut into even-sized pieces
4 tablespoons mayonnaise, or 2 tablespoons mayonnaise and 2 tablespoons plain yogurt or soured cream, or tofu dressing (page 199) or 1 quantity vinaigrette (page 110) for vegans
salt and freshly ground black pepper
chopped fresh parsley or chives (optional)

Cook the potatoes in water to cover them until they are only just tender, then drain immediately. Let the potatoes cool slightly, cut them into smaller pieces, if you wish, and put them into a bowl. Add the dressing of your choice, salt and pepper to taste and stir gently until the potato is coated with the dressing. Put the salad in a bowl and snip a little parsley or chives on top, if you like. Cool completely before serving.

Tomato Salad ◕ Ⓥ

Although this salad is very quickly prepared, it does improve in flavour if you can leave it standing for about 30 minutes before serving.

Serves 4

700 g (1½ lb) firm tomatoes — beefsteak tomatoes can be used
1–2 tablespoons olive oil
salt and freshly ground black pepper
chopped fresh basil if available

The tomatoes can be used with their skin on, or you can remove it, depending on the state of the tomatoes and on your personal taste. To skin the tomatoes, place them in a bowl, pour on boiling water to cover them, leave for a minute or two, until the skins are loose enough to pull off, then drain the tomatoes immediately and put them in cold water. Remove the skins with a sharp knife.

Slice the tomatoes into circles or slim segments, discarding any tough part around the stalk end. Put the tomatoes in a bowl, sprinkle with the olive oil, some salt and pepper, and the basil if you have some. Then, if possible, leave for 30 minutes or longer, stirring gently occasionally, to give the flavours time to blend.

VARIATION

Tomato and Onion Salad

Make as described above, but add 1–2 mild sweet onions, peeled and cut into thin slices.

Green Salad ◕ Ⓥ

This is probably the recipe that I use more than any other, as a green salad is an almost standard accompaniment to most dishes in our house, and certainly one of my favourites. But the basic mixture always seems to be different, depending on what crisp, fresh green salad vegetables and herbs are available. The possibilities are endless in summer when there are not only many fresh herbs around but also such delicacies as rocket, sorrel, dandelion leaves and nasturtium leaves and flowers.

But even in winter the interesting bitter-leaf salad items such as chicory, oakleaf lettuce and radicchio can turn a green salad into a lively affair, and it's surprising how a little of some of the hardier herbs such as thyme and rosemary, and sliced onion or tender spinach leaves, plus a good tasty vinaigrette, can jazz up even a plain floppy hot-house lettuce. The only leaves that I find rather dull and uninspiring are Chinese leaves, which seem to have got more boring as they have become more widely available.

Serves 4

vinaigrette (page 110)
1 lettuce
other leafy items as available: watercress, a head or two of chicory, or one of radicchio; a few leaves of rocket, sorrel, tender spinach, nasturtium or dandelion
1–2 or more tablespoons chopped fresh herbs as available — parsley, chives, mint, fennel, dill, tarragon; or 1–2 teaspoons more pungent herbs such as rosemary and thyme
other items such as finely sliced onion, chopped spring onion, to taste

Make the vinaigrette as described, straight into a salad bowl, adding garlic if you like this flavour. Then cross a pair of salad servers in the base of the bowl and put the salad leaves on top, to prevent the lower leaves from getting into the dressing and becoming soggy. Turn the salad in the dressing just before you want to serve it (I usually do this at the table) so that all the leaves are coated in the dressing but still crisp.

Pretty Carrot Salad ◐ Ⓥ

Grated carrot makes a good basis for year-round salads which are useful for serving with dishes when you want something fresh and colourful. I've suggested some vegetables in the recipe but, along with the carrot, many different ones can be used: chopped red pepper, fresh raw or cooked sweetcorn (and the little baby corn cobs), celery, spring onions and cherry tomatoes are other possibilities.

Serves 4

vinaigrette (page 110)
4 medium-large carrots, scraped and coarsely grated
bunch of radishes, washed, trimmed and sliced, or cut into
    flowers if you have time
1 carton of cress, trimmed and washed

Make the vinaigrette straight into a bowl, add the rest of the ingredients and mix gently.

Cucumber, Radish and Hiziki Salad ◑ Ⓥ

A pretty, nutritious salad with a Japanese flavour. You can buy hiziki seaweed and rice vinegar, which has a particularly delicate, slightly sweet flavour, at some health shops and stockists of Japanese foods.

Serves 4

small handful of hiziki
1 cucumber
1 bunch of radishes
1–2 tablespoons rice vinegar or wine vinegar
sugar, salt and freshly ground black pepper

Wash the hiziki, then put it in a saucepan, cover with water, and simmer for 5–15 minutes, until it has softened enough for your taste. Drain. Meanwhile, peel and dice the cucumber; wash, trim and slice the radishes. Put the cucumber and radishes into a bowl, add the hiziki, vinegar and sugar, salt and pepper to taste and mix well.

Vitality Salad Bowl ◑ Ⓥ

This is a wonderful, crunchy salad, which makes a filling lunch.

Serves 1

2–3 lettuce leaves, washed and shredded
2–3 tablespoons canned red kidney beans, drained
2–3 tablespoons cooked brown rice or diced potato
1 tomato, chopped
5 cm/2 inches cucumber, diced
a few beansprouts, if available
1 carrot, coarsely grated
1 small raw beetroot, peeled and grated
1 tablespoon mayonnaise or plain yogurt, or tofu dressing (page 201) or 1–2 tablespoons home-made vinaigrette (page 110) for vegans
a little salad cress to garnish

Put all the salad ingredients into a deep bowl — a soup bowl is ideal — top with the mayonnaise, yogurt or vinaigrette, sprinkle the cress on top of that, and serve.

Cream Cheese Roll Salad

Serves 2–4

100 g (4 oz) walnuts or hazel nuts
125 g (4 oz) cream or curd cheese
½ teaspoon paprika pepper
2 tablespoons chopped chives
salt and freshly ground black pepper
1 small lettuce
2 carrots, coarsely grated
1–2 tomatoes, sliced
1 box cress, trimmed and washed
a few radishes, sliced or cut into roses

If you are using hazel nuts and the dark brown skins are still intact, spread the nuts out on a dry baking sheet and bake them at 190°C/375°F/Gas Mark 5, for about 20 minutes, until the skins loosen and the nuts underneath are golden brown. Rub off the skins. Grind the nuts.

Put the cream or curd cheese into a bowl, beat a little to soften it, then mix in the nuts, paprika pepper, chopped chives and some salt and pepper to taste. Form the mixture into a roll, wrap in foil, and pop the roll into the fridge for about 30 minutes to chill. Then cut the roll into slices and arrange on a base of lettuce on a serving plate, or on individual plates. Place the other salad ingredients attractively around the slices of roll.

Bulgur Wheat Salad ◑ Ⓥ

Serves 8

225 g (8 oz) bulgur wheat
1 teaspoon salt
350 ml (12 fl oz) boiling water
450 g (1 lb) tomatoes
½ cucumber
50 ml (2 fl oz) olive oil
50 ml (2 fl oz) lemon juice
2 garlic cloves, peeled and crushed
3 tablespoons finely chopped fresh mint
3 tablespoons finely chopped parsley
1 cos lettuce, to serve

Put the bulgur wheat in a bowl with the salt and add the boiling water. Leave for 15 minutes, for the wheat to absorb the water.

Meanwhile skin the tomatoes: cover them with boiling water, leave for 1–2 minutes, rinse in cold water, then slip off the skins. Chop the tomatoes. Cut the cucumber into 5 mm/¼ inch dice.

Add the oil, lemon juice, garlic, mint and parsley to the wheat and stir well, then add the tomatoes and cucumber.

Line a serving dish with cos lettuce leaves and pile the salad on top.

Colourful Bean Salad ◑ Ⓥ

Bean salads can be made from any mixture of beans, and
you can keep to simple colour schemes or achieve vivid
technicolour effects by using several contrasting types of bean
and bright ingredients such as sweetcorn, chopped red pepper
and black olives or raisins. Here's one of the colourful variety.
Serve it with some warm wholewheat rolls or crusty bread,
and perhaps some green salad, for a complete meal.

Serves 6

1 tablespoon Dijon mustard
1 tablespoon wine vinegar
3 tablespoons olive oil
salt and freshly ground black pepper
425 g (15 oz) can cannellini or butter beans, drained
425 g (15 oz) can red kidney beans, drained
125 g (4 oz) sweetcorn: fresh raw kernels cut from a cob,
or frozen sweetcorn, thawed
12 black olives, halved and stoned, or 50 g (2 oz) raisins
1 small red pepper, de-seeded and finely chopped
2 heaped tablespoons chopped parsley

Put the mustard, vinegar and oil into a large bowl with some
salt and pepper and mix together, to make an emulsion. Then
add all the remaining ingredients and mix gently together.

6. Vegetables

The important things to remember when cooking vegetables are that the vegetables should be as fresh as possible, have as little cut away from them as possible and be cooked in as little water as possible for the shortest time possible! I've found that the longer I've been cooking, the less time I've been giving vegetables to cook, and now I like even boiled potatoes rather under-done, still with some 'bite' to them. This may not be to everyone's taste, but vegetables are certainly best if they're crisp and veering on being too little cooked, rather than over-cooked.

When you are calculating the amount of vegetables you need, allow about 175 g (6 oz) for each person (weighed before preparation) or 225 g (8 oz) where there is a lot of waste, as in spinach and leafy leeks, and 450 g (1 lb) for peas and beans in their pods.

As a general rule, potatoes and similar root vegetables are best cooked in water just to cover, and this can be cold to start with. Other vegetables are nicest when cooked in just enough water to prevent the pan from burning dry — about 1 cm/½ inch for 700–900 g (1½–2 lb) — and this should be boiling when the vegetables are put in. I always put a lid on the pan, so that the vegetables above the water are in fact cooking in the steam — steaming, rather than boiling. In my experience, this gives excellent results. The vegetables are done when they can be pierced with a fine skewer or the point of a slim sharp knife; then strain off the water immediately, add a little butter or vegetable margarine, if you like, a grinding of black pepper and a little sea salt unless you cooked them in salted water. I prefer to cook them in plain water and either salt them before serving, or serve them as they are, so that people can add it themselves if they like it.

Well cooked vegetables don't need many additions, but some chopped fresh herbs, or a squeeze of fresh lemon juice can be pleasant, and sometimes a little cream or soured cream.

Artichokes

Globe

Allow one per person. Break off the stem level with the base. Snip off the points of the leaves. Wash the artichokes well. Bring a large panful of water to the boil (use an enamel or steel pan, as aluminium reacts with artichokes), put the artichokes in so that they are fully immersed, then let them simmer for 30–45 minutes, or until one of the base leaves will pull away easily. Turn the artichokes upside down to drain.

Serve the artichokes with melted butter. Peel off the leaves one by one, dip the fleshy base in melted butter, eat, and discard the rest of the leaf. When you reach the central hairy choke, cut this out and discard it; then cut up the tender base of the artichoke and eat it with the remaining butter.

If you are preparing artichokes for guests, you might prefer to pull back the spiky leaves and cut out the hairy choke before cooking the artichokes, to avoid having to do this at the table.

Artichokes are also delicious cooked and served cold, as a starter, with a pool of vinaigrette or some mayonnaise poured into the central space where the choke was.

Jerusalem

Peel, cutting off some of the nobbles if peeling round them is too intricate. Then put them into an enamel or stainless steel saucepan, cover with water and boil for about 20 minutes, until tender. Or put them into a heavy based pan with 15 g ($\frac{1}{2}$ oz) butter, 4 tablespoons water and a little salt, and cook over a low heat until just tender, about 20 minutes. Grind a little pepper over them.

Asparagus

Break off the thick stalk ends, then peel upwards to make the base the same width as the upper stem. Wash the asparagus well to remove any grit which sometimes lodges itself in the tips. Tie the stems in a bundle, stand this in a saucepan containing 2.5 cm/1 inch of boiling water. Cover the pan with a dome of foil if the height of the asparagus makes it impossible to get a lid on the pan. Boil for 8–15 minutes, until the asparagus is tender. Serve with melted butter.

Aubergines

Remove the stalks carefully as they contain tiny prickles which can get into your hands. Then slice or cube the aubergine and put it into a colander. Sprinkle with salt, put a plate and a weight on top, and leave for 30 minutes. This draws out the brown liquid — which can be bitter — and softens the aubergine, so that it doesn't absorb so much oil when you cook it. Rinse the aubergine under cold water, squeeze dry. Fry in a little oil for about 5 minutes, or until tender.

Beansprouts

Wash, drain and stir-fry in 1–2 tablespoons oil for 1–2 minutes, until heated through but still crisp.

Beetroot

Cut off the leaves, if still attached, 10 cm/4 inches above the beetroot and don't cut or peel the beetroot — both precautions against the colour draining out. Cover the beetroot with cold water, then boil for 1–3 hours, until tender. Slip the skins off the beetroot, then slice or cube the beetroot and reheat in a little butter.

Broad Beans

If they are young and tender, they can be just topped and tailed and cooked like French beans. Older ones need to be popped out of their pods, then simmered in boiling water to cover until tender, 5–10 minutes. Drain and serve with butter and pepper or chopped herbs.

Broccoli and Calabrese

Cut off the thick, less tender stems and slice these into matchsticks. Bring 2.5 cm/1 inch of water to the boil, put in the matchsticks and simmer for a couple of minutes, then add the tender florets, and simmer until just tender, 2–5 minutes. Drain thoroughly.

Brussels Sprouts

Choose small firm ones if possible. Trim off the outer leaves and stalk ends. Cook really tiny ones whole in a little boiling water; halve or quarter larger ones. Boil until just tender, 2–5 minutes. Drain well.

Cabbage

Trim off the outer leaves, quarter the cabbage, then shred, removing the central core. Boil for 5–7 minutes; drain well, swirl with melted butter and grated black pepper.

Carrots

Scrub tender carrots; scrape or peel older ones. Leave small carrots whole; halve, quarter, slice or dice larger ones. Boil in water to cover for 5–10 minutes, until tender.

Cauliflower

Break into florets, trim off tough stems. Boil for 3–5 minutes drain very well.

Celeriac

Peel fairly thickly, cut into even sized chunks. Boil in a stainless steel or enamel pan for 30–40 minutes. Serve with butter; or mash with butter and a little of the cooking water, milk or cream, to make a purée. A little mashed potato is good added to a celeriac purée.

Celery

Choose small compact hearts and wash them well. Trim to about 15 cm/6 inches, halve or quarter lengthwise. Or use the outer stalks of celery only; trim and cut into even-sized lengths. Melt 15 g (½ oz) butter in a flameproof casserole and put in the celery, a small sliced onion, a bay leaf, little salt and pepper, and 100 ml (4 fl oz) water. Bring to the boil, then bake at 180°C/350°F/Gas Mark 4 for 1–1¼ hours, or until the celery is tender.

Chicory

Remove damaged leaves, trim base. Insert the point of a knife in the base and twist to remove a cone-shaped 'core'; this reduces bitterness and ensures even cooking. Cook in butter and a very little water as described for Jerusalem artichokes.

Chinese Cabbage, Chinese Leaves

Trim, shred finely and stir-fry in 2–4 tablespoons oil in a large saucepan or wok for 2–3 minutes, until just heated through. Season. A little chopped onion can be stir-fried with the leaves for extra flavour, or some fresh herbs can be added at the end of the cooking.

Courgettes

Top and tail finger-sized courgettes; slice, dice or coarsely grate older ones. Fry in a little butter, or boil until barely tender, perhaps for only 1-2 minutes, drain well and serve with butter and fresh herbs.

Fennel

Trim off stalk ends, base and any tough outer leaves. Boil and serve with butter, or braise as described for celery.

French Beans

Top and tail; leave whole or cut large ones into shorter lengths, then boil in a small amount of water for 2–10 minutes, depending on size. Don't overcook them; they're lovely with plenty of crunch left in them.

Kale

Remove stalks, pulling leaves away from the stem. Boil in 1 cm/½ inch of water for 5–7 minutes; drain well.

Kohlrabi

Prepare and cook as for swede.

Leeks

Cut off roots and most of the green part; slit down one side and rinse out the grit under running water. Leave whole, or slice. Cook as described for Jerusalem artichokes. Alternatively, boil until tender: 2–5 minutes for sliced leeks, 8–15 minutes for thin whole leeks. Drain well.

Mangetout Peas

Prepare as for French beans. Stir-fry in a little oil for 1–2 minutes, or boil for the same amount of time. They should still be crunchy.

Marrow

Cut off stem, halve, peel and cut marrow into even-sized pieces. Remove seeds if tough. Cook as described for Jerusalem artichokes.

Mushrooms

Peel field mushrooms, wash but don't peel cultivated ones, trim and wash wild mushrooms if you're lucky enough to have these. Leave small ones whole, slice large ones. Trim stalks off flat open mushrooms. Fry in butter or oil until tender. If they give off some liquid, either drain, reserving the liquid for stock, or, for the best flavour, increase the heat and cook them hard until the liquid has boiled away. Flat mushrooms are good brushed with oil and grilled.

Okra

Top and tail; cook gently in 3–4 tablespoons oil for about 20 minutes, perhaps with a sliced onion, tomato and 1–2 teaspoons ground coriander. Season with salt and pepper.

Onions

These are good baked in their skins at 200°C/400°F/Gas Mark 6 for about 1 hour. When they are done, split them and serve with butter, salt and pepper; or peel, cut into even-sized pieces and boil for 5–15 minutes, until tender; or fry in butter or oil for about 10 minutes, until tender.

Parsnips

Prepare as for swede. Mash with butter and serve, or roast in oil, like roast potatoes (page 127).

Peas

Shell, boil for 5–10 minutes. Or put into a heavy-based saucepan with the washed and chopped outside leaves of a large lettuce, 15 g (½ oz) butter, ½ teaspoon sugar and some salt and pepper, and simmer over a moderate heat, with a lid on the pan, for 15–20 minutes. This is an excellent way of bringing the best out of frozen peas, and they only need about 7–8 minutes cooking time. Serve the lettuce leaves with the peas.

Peppers

Halve, removing the stalks, core and seeds, then slice. Fry in oil for about 15 minutes, or until softened. Or cook under a hot grill until the outer skin wrinkles and can be rinsed off, leaving the tender, sweet inner flesh. For stuffed peppers, see page 71.

Potatoes

Scrape or peel potatoes, or scrub the skins and leave them on. Boil in water to cover until tender and serve with butter, or mash with butter and milk or cream until light and fluffy.

For chips, cut potatoes into slices, put one of these into a deep-frying pan one-third full of oil. When it starts to sizzle, add the rest and cook until golden; the longer they fry, the crisper they will get. Drain and serve immediately.

For roast potatoes, put 5mm/¼ inch of oil into a roasting tin and put into the oven to heat up: the oven should be heated to 200–230°C/400–450°F/Gas Mark 6–8. Meanwhile, boil potatoes for 5–7 minutes. Drain the potatoes and put the hot potatoes straight into the sizzling hot oil. Quickly turn the potatoes in the oil then put them in the oven and bake for about 45 minutes, until golden and crisp, turning them once or twice during this time. If they are cooking too quickly, turn the heat down to 160°C/325°F/Gas Mark 3 until you are ready to serve them. Drain the potatoes well on kitchen paper.

Bircher potatoes are an excellent variation, a kind of cross between roast potatoes and jacket potatoes. Scrub the potatoes, cut them in half, then put them cut-side down on an oiled baking sheet. Bake at 200°C/400°F/Gas Mark 6 for 45–60 minutes, until the potatoes are soft and the cut sides are golden brown and crisp.

Pumpkin

Prepare and cook as for marrow.

Red Cabbage

Shred 700–900 g (1½–2 lb) red cabbage. Fry 2 large chopped onions in 3 tablespoons oil in a flameproof pan for 5–10 minutes, then put in the cabbage, with 1½ teaspoons salt, 1 teaspoon sugar, 2 tablespoons wine vinegar, ½ teaspoon cinnamon, a pinch of ground cloves and some freshly grated black pepper. Cover with a lid and cook very gently on top of the stove for 1½ hours, or for about 2 hours at 160°C/325°F/Gas Mark 3. Stir from time to time, to help the mixture to cook evenly.

Runner Beans

Top and tail; cut down the sides of the beans to remove any tough strings, if necessary. Cut the beans into 2.5 cm/1 inch pieces or slice them in a bean slicer. Boil for 5–10 minutes until just tender.

Salsify and Scorzonera

Scrape, keeping roots submerged. Cut into even-sized pieces, boil in water to cover in a stainless steel or enamel saucepan for 5–15 minutes, until tender.

Spinach

Wash very thoroughly. Remove stalks or keep them on, for added flavour and texture. Put the spinach in a large saucepan with no extra water. As the spinach boils down, chop it with the end of a fish slice and turn it so that it cooks evenly. Drain and serve with butter, salt and black pepper.

Swede

Peel thickly, cut into even-sized pieces, cover with water and boil for 15–20 minutes, until tender. Mash with butter and seasoning.

Sweet Potatoes

Scrub, cut into pieces, and bake like potatoes (page 10), or peel, boil and purée.

Sweetcorn

Remove leaves and silky threads, trim off stalk. Immerse in a large panful of boiling unsalted water, simmer for about 10 minutes, until the kernels are tender. Don't overcook, or they toughen. Drain and serve with melted butter. To cook just the kernels, cut these from the husk, then cook in boiling water for 2–5 minutes.

Swiss Chard

Strip leaves from stems and cook as for spinach. Cut stems into 10 cm/4 inch lengths, boil for 4–5 minutes, until just tender. Drain and serve with melted butter.

Tomatoes

Remove stalks, cut a cross in the top of the tomatoes and bake at 180°C/350°F/Gas Mark 4, for 10–15 minutes. Or halve and fry on both sides; or halve, dot with butter and bake or grill for 10 minutes.

Turnips

Peel; leave baby turnips whole; halve or quarter larger ones. Boil for 5–10 minutes, drain well, return to pan and dry out over heat. Serve with butter, or mash to a purée, perhaps adding a little mashed potato for extra body.

RECIPES

Ratatouille V

This is a useful vegetable recipe because it goes well with many savoury dishes and, because it is moist, can substitute as a sauce. Ratatouille makes a good, light main course, too, served with cooked brown rice or crusty bread; and cold, it's good as a salad.

Serves 4

450 g (1 lb) aubergines, diced
salt
3 tablespoons olive oil
2 large onions, peeled and chopped
3 large red peppers, de-seeded and chopped
1 garlic clove, peeled and crushed
450 g (1 lb) courgettes, washed and sliced
700 g (1½ lb) tomatoes, skinned and chopped
freshly ground black pepper

Put the aubergines in a colander, sprinkle with salt, put a plate and a weight on top, and leave for 30 minutes. Then rinse well and squeeze as dry as possible. Heat the oil in a large saucepan and fry the onions and peppers gently for 5 minutes. Then add the garlic, courgettes and aubergines. Stir, then cover and cook gently for about 25 minutes, or until the vegetables are tender. Add the tomatoes and cook gently, uncovered, for about 5 minutes, until heated through. Season with salt and freshly ground black pepper.

Spiced Leeks ◑ Ⅴ

A particularly delicious way to cook leeks.

Serves 4

6 leeks
1 tablespoon olive oil
150 ml (¼ pint) wine, white or red
2 bay leaves
1 teaspoon pickling spice, wrapped in a piece of gauze
salt and freshly ground black pepper

Trim the roots from the leeks and cut off all but about 2 cm/1 inch of the green part. Then slit the leeks down one side and wash carefully under cold water. Cut the leeks into 2 cm/1 inch lengths. Heat the oil in a medium saucepan and add the leeks; fry for 2–3 minutes, then add the wine, bay leaves, pickling spice and a little salt and pepper. Bring to the boil, then cover and cook gently for about 20 minutes, or until the leeks are tender. Remove pickling spice, check seasoning, and serve.

Spiced Potatoes ◑ Ⓥ ♀

This is delicious as a side-dish with a curry, to accompany a lentil or nut roast, or with Falafel (page 43), a yogurt sauce and one or two salads; or packed into pitta pockets, along with some sliced tomatoes, for a spicy snack.

Serves 4

2 tablespoons oil
1 onion, peeled and chopped
900 g (2 lb) potatoes, peeled and cut into 1 cm/½ inch dice
1 garlic clove, peeled and crushed
½ teaspoon turmeric
1 teaspoon ground coriander
2 cardamom pods
salt and freshly ground black pepper
150 ml (5 fl oz) water
1–2 tablespoons fresh coriander, chopped (optional)

Heat the oil in a medium saucepan, then add the onion and fry for 7–8 minutes, with a lid on the pan, stirring from time to time. Then add the potatoes, garlic, turmeric, coriander, cardamom and some salt and pepper. Stir well over the heat, to distribute all the ingredients, then add the water. Bring to the boil, then put a lid on the pan and turn the heat down as low as you can. Leave to cook for about 10 minutes, or until the potatoes are just tender and most of the water has been absorbed. Check the seasoning, then sprinkle with fresh coriander, if available, and serve.

Red Cabbage Casserole Ⓥ

This casserole is very quickly prepared but needs to cook for a long time. It can be made in advance and reheated; it tastes even better the next day; it also tastes good cold.

Serves 4–6

1 red cabbage, about 1 kg (2¼ lb)
2 tablespoons oil
1 large onion, peeled and chopped
2 tablespoons lemon juice
salt and freshly ground black pepper
sugar

Cut the cabbage into quarters and remove the central core and any tough stems, then shred the cabbage and rinse under cold water. Next, put the cabbage into a large saucepan, cover with water, and bring to the boil, then drain thoroughly.

Heat the oil in a large saucepan and fry the onion for 5 minutes, then add the cabbage, lemon juice, some salt and pepper and stir well. Cover, and cook gently for 45–60 minutes, or until the cabbage is very tender, stirring from time to time. Check the seasoning, adding a dash of sugar to taste if you think the mixture needs it.

Parsnip and Celery Cream ◑ ♀

The flavours and textures of the parsnips and celery complement each other particularly well.

Serves 4

25 g (1 oz) butter
1 onion, peeled and chopped
700 g (1½ lb) parsnips, peeled and cut into 1 cm/½ inch dice
1 head of celery, washed, trimmed and chopped
150 ml (5 fl oz) water
salt and freshly ground black pepper
3–4 tablespoons double cream
freshly grated nutmeg

Melt the butter in a heavy-based saucepan, then add the onion and fry for 5 minutes, without browning. Add the parsnips and celery; stir well, then pour in the water and add some salt and pepper to taste. Bring to the boil, then put a lid on the pan, turn the heat right down, and leave to cook gently for about 30 minutes, or until the vegetables are tender. Check the seasoning, stir in the cream, grate in a little nutmeg, and serve.

7. Sauces

Vegetarian Gravy ◔ Ⓥ

This is my daughter Margaret's recipe for a particularly tasty vegetarian gravy.

Serves 4–6

2 tablespoons oil
2 tablespoons (1 oz) flour
4 teaspoons gravy powder (such as Bisto — but read the list of ingredients, as some types have meat in, others don't)
600 ml (1 pint) water
1 teaspoon Marmite
1 teaspoon vegetarian stock
1 bay leaf
salt and freshly ground black pepper

Heat the oil in a medium saucepan then add the flour and stir over the heat for a few minutes until the flour is nut-brown. Add the gravy powder, then pour in the water, stirring all the time. Add the Marmite, vegetarian stock and bay leaf. Let the gravy simmer for about 10 minutes, to cook the flour, then it's ready.

Tomato Sauce ◐ Ⅴ

Serves 4

1 tablespoon olive oil
1 onion, peeled and chopped
450 g (1 lb) tomatoes, or 425 g (15 oz) can tomatoes
1 large garlic glove, peeled and crushed
1 teaspoon dried basil
salt and freshly ground black pepper

Heat the oil in a medium saucepan and fry the onion for 5 minutes with a lid on the pan. Chop the tomatoes roughly — there's no need to skin fresh ones — then add to the onion with the garlic and the basil. Mix well, then put a lid on the pan and simmer for 15–20 minutes. If you used canned tomatoes, the sauce can be used as it is, or liquidized; if you used fresh tomatoes, liquidize the sauce then pour it through a sieve into a clean pan, to remove the tomato skins. Season with salt and pepper.

White Sauce ◐

Serves 4

Makes 600 ml/1 pint

50 g (2 oz) butter
40g (1½ oz) plain flour
600 ml (1 pint) milk
salt and freshly ground black pepper

Melt the butter in a medium saucepan, then add the flour. Stir over the heat for a moment, then add a third of the milk. Stir until thick, then stir in another third and stir again. Repeat with the final third, stirring until the sauce is smooth. Leave the sauce to cook over a very gentle heat for 10 minutes, then remove from the heat and season with salt and pepper to taste.

VARIATIONS

Béchamel Sauce

Serves 4

This is a delicately flavoured white sauce. To make it, you first flavour the milk. To do this, put the milk in a saucepan with a small piece of peeled raw onion, a piece of scraped carrot, a celery stick if you have one, a bay leaf and a few parsley stalks and sprigs of thyme, if available. Bring to the boil, then remove from the heat, cover and leave for at least 15 minutes, for the flavours to infuse. Then strain, discard the vegetables and herbs, and use the milk to make a sauce as described above.

Cheese Sauce

Serves 4

For cheese sauce, make a white sauce as described above. When it has simmered for 10 minutes, remove from the heat and stir in 50–100 g (2–4 oz) strongly flavoured grated cheese (such as mature Cheddar) and a good pinch of dried mustard or cayenne pepper.

Cranberry Sauce ◔ V

Serves 4

175 g (6 oz) fresh cranberries
4 tablespoons water
75 g (3 oz) sugar
grated rind and juice of 1 well-scrubbed orange

Rinse the cranberries and remove any damaged ones. Put the cranberries into a saucepan with the water, cover with a lid and cook gently for 4–5 minutes, until the cranberries are tender. Then add the sugar and cook over a low heat until the granules have dissolved. Remove from the heat and add the orange rind and juice. The mixture will thicken as it cools. Reheat gently before serving.

Bread Sauce

This sauce is very easy and quick to prepare but the mixture needs to stand for 1–2 hours before breadcrumbs are added, to allow flavours to infuse.

Serves 6–8

8 cloves
1 onion, peeled
1 bay leaf
300 ml (10 fl oz) milk
50 g (2 oz) soft white breadcrumbs
15 g (½ oz) butter
2 tablespoons double cream
salt and freshly ground pepper
freshly grated nutmeg

Stick the cloves in the onion and put this into a saucepan with the bay leaf and milk. Bring to the boil, then remove from the heat, cover and leave for 1–2 hours for the flavours to infuse. Then add the breadcrumbs and butter and mix well. Cover, and leave until just before you are ready to serve, then remove the onion and bay leaf. Stir in the cream and some salt, pepper and freshly grated nutmeg to taste.

Soured Cream and Herb Sauce ◑

This is a useful sauce for serving cold with hot nut or lentil roast or burgers, or with vegetable pasties.

Serves 4–6

150 ml (5 fl oz) soured cream
1–2 tablespoons chopped fresh herbs, such as parsley, mint, basil or dill
salt and freshly ground black pepper

Put the soured cream in a bowl and mix in the herbs. Season to taste with salt and pepper. Pour into a small jug or bowl to serve.

Yogurt and Cucumber Sauce ◕

Another useful sauce for serving cold with hot nut or lentil roast or burgers, or with vegetable pasties.

Serves 4–6

150 ml (5 fl oz) yogurt
5 cm/2 inches cucumber, peeled and finely diced
salt and freshly ground black pepper

Put the yogurt in a bowl and mix in the cucumber. Season to taste with salt and pepper. Pour into a small jug or bowl to serve.

8. Puddings

COLD PUDDINGS

A colourful selection of fresh fruit, attractively arranged, perhaps on a base of fresh leaves, makes the easiest pudding, and is pleasant and healthy. Or you can take this a step further, and arrange a platter of fresh fruits with other colourful treats such as sugared almonds, crystallized fruits, turkish delight, chocolate, wheatmeal biscuits and some little cheeses, fresh shelled nuts . . . whatever takes your fancy.

When there's a little more time, many quick — simply delicious — puddings can be made from fruit, yogurt, cream and some of the new low-fat soft white cheeses; or some good cheese, like a piece of mature farmhouse Cheddar, with crusty French bread, wholewheat crackers, or crisp celery or slices of mellow apple, makes a very pleasant ending to a meal.

Here are some recipes for cold puddings, many of which can be made in advance and kept in the fridge or freezer until needed.

Exotic Fruit Salad

You can use any mixture of interesting exotic fruits to make this fruit salad, but I think this mixture of white lychees, golden star fruit (or tangerines) and green kiwi fruit is particularly attractive; or, alternatively, pink guava, black grapes and green kiwi fruit.

Serves 4

400 g (14 oz) can lychees or guavas
2 kiwi fruits
2 star fruits or 2 large (or 4 small) tangerines

Place lychees or guavas, with juice, in a serving bowl. Peel kiwi fruits over bowl, so juices run into it; slice and add to bowl. Peel star fruits or tangerines over bowl, divide into segments and add to bowl. Mix well.

Fresh Date Salad with Yogurt and Honey

One of Prue Leith's delicious ideas, excellent when made with big juicy fresh dates, thick creamy Greek yogurt and the best honey and cream.

Serves 4

450 g (1 lb) fresh dates
200 g (7 oz) carton strained Greek yogurt
150 ml (5 fl oz) double cream, preferably Jersey
4 tablespoons clear honey, preferably Greek

Halve the dates, removing the stones, then put them into four individual bowls. Spoon some yogurt on top of the dates, dividing it between the bowls, then pour the cream and honey over the top. Serve at once.

Pears in Red Wine ♀

These are good served with some lightly whipped cream and some buttery shortbread biscuits.

Serves 4

4 firm dessert pears
50 g (2 oz) sugar
300 ml (10 fl oz) red wine
300 ml (10 fl oz) water

Peel the pears, leaving them whole, but don't remove the stalks. Put the sugar in a saucepan with the wine and water and heat gently until the sugar has dissolved, then bring to the boil. Add the pears, cover and simmer gently for 40 minutes, or until the pears are tender right through to the centres. Don't undercook them, or the inside will turn brown. When the pears are done, remove them from the pan with a slotted spoon and place them in a serving dish. Boil the liquid in the pan vigorously until it has reduced by half, then pour this over the pears. Cool, then chill.

Peaches in Wine ♀

Another simple fruit dish, different from the last one, but equally good and suitable for a special occasion. It is quick to prepare but needs to be chilled for at least 30 minutes before serving.

Serves 4

4 large ripe peaches
1 rounded tablespoon caster sugar
120 ml (4 fl oz) sweet white wine

Skin the peaches: put them in a deep bowl, cover them with boiling water and leave for 2–3 minutes, until you can slip the skins off easily with a pointed knife. At this point drain the peaches, then remove all the skins. Slice the peaches, removing the stones. Put the slices in a glass bowl, or individual serving dishes, and sprinkle with the sugar. Pour the wine over the peaches, then chill for at least 30 minutes, or until needed.

Dried Fruit Compote ♀

This is quick and easy to make, but you need to allow time for the fruit to soak overnight, and then to cook slowly. It's good served with some chilled thick, creamy strained Greek yogurt (for non-vegans). As you can see from the recipe, it can be jazzed up in various ways, depending on your mood, purse and who you're making it for!

Serves 4–6

450 g (1 lb) dried fruit salad mixture (containing dried apricots, peaches, apples etc)
1 cinnamon stick (optional)
50 g (2 oz) crystallized ginger, chopped (optional)
2–4 tablespoons brandy (optional)

Rinse the fruit quickly under running water, then put into a bowl with the cinnamon stick, if you're using this, and cover with water. Leave to soak overnight, or for 6–8 hours. Then transfer the whole lot to a saucepan, and simmer gently, with a lid on the pan, for 30 minutes, or until the fruit is very tender. Take the lid off the pan towards the end of the cooking time to allow the liquid to boil away a bit, so that it becomes syrupy. Then remove from the heat and add the ginger and brandy, if you wish. Cool, then chill. Remove the cinnamon stick before serving.

Easy Yogurt Pudding ♀

A special pudding that can be made in minutes, but it needs to be chilled before serving.

Serves 6

300 ml (10 fl oz) double cream
300 ml (10 fl oz) plain yogurt
1 teaspoon cinnamon
1 teaspoon lemon juice
125–225 g (4–8 oz) soft brown sugar

Whip the cream until it stands in stiff peaks, then gently stir in the yogurt, cinnamon and lemon juice. Spoon the mixture into a glass serving dish, or individual dishes and cover the top with an even layer of soft brown sugar. Chill until needed.

Nectarines with a Cream Topping ♀

Another delicious special occasion pudding which can be made quickly and easily, though you do need to start it the night before. The combination of the chilled cream and fruit and the hot melted sugar is delicious.

Serves 4-6

900 g (2 lb) ripe nectarines
1 rounded teaspoon caster sugar
3–4 tablespoons brandy
300 ml (10 fl oz) double cream
125–225 g (4–8 oz) soft brown sugar

Skin the nectarines: put them in a deep bowl, cover them with boiling water and leave for 2–3 minutes, until you can slip the skins off easily with a pointed knife. Slice the nectarines, removing the stones. Put the slices into a flameproof bowl and sprinkle with the sugar and brandy. Whip the cream until it stands in stiff peaks, then spoon this on top of the nectarines, smoothing it level, to cover the fruit completely. Sprinkle the brown sugar over the top in an even layer. Chill overnight. Just before you want to serve the pudding, heat the grill. Put the pudding under the grill for a few minutes, so that the sugar melts and caramelizes slightly.

Old English Trifle ♀

This is a little trouble to make, with its delicate real egg custard, but it can be made well in advance and the delight which it usually provokes makes the effort worthwhile!

Serves 6

8 trifle sponges, or one layer of a sponge cake
100–175 g (4–6 oz) raspberry jam
100 g (4 oz) macaroons, lightly crushed
100 ml (4 fl oz) medium sherry or sweet white wine

For the custard

600 ml (1 pint) milk
2 tablespoons caster sugar
1 vanilla pod
4 egg yolks
1 teaspoon cornflour

To finish

150 ml (5 fl oz) double cream
50 g (2 oz) flaked almonds, toasted

Spread the cake or trifle sponges with the jam, cut into pieces and put in a 2-litre/3½-pint glass serving bowl with the macaroons. Sprinkle the sherry or wine over the top and leave to soak for about 2 hours.

Meanwhile, make the custard. Put the milk in a medium saucepan with the sugar and vanilla pod and bring to the boil. Immediately remove the saucepan from the heat. Remove the vanilla pod (which can be thoroughly rinsed, then dried and kept for re-use). Mix the egg yolks together in a bowl with the cornflour. Pour on the scalded milk, stirring, then return the mixture to the saucepan. Stir over a gentle heat until the mixture thickens enough to coat the back of the spoon. Do not let the custard get too hot or it will curdle. Pour into a clean bowl and leave to cool.

To finish the trifle, pour the custard over the cake mixture. Whip the cream, then spread over the custard, and top with the flaked almonds. Chill until needed.

Strawberry Shortbread

Serves 6
A pretty dessert for a special summer meal.

225 g (8 oz) strawberries
50 g (2 oz) caster sugar
300 ml (10 fl oz) double cream

For the shortbread

175 g (6 oz) butter
75 g (3 oz) caster sugar
175 g (6 oz) plain flour, white, 85% wholewheat or 100% wholewheat, sifted
75 g (3 oz) ground rice

Set the oven to 180°C/350°F/Gas Mark 4. First make the shortbread. Beat the butter until soft and fluffy, then beat in the sugar. Stir in the flour until well mixed, then stir in the ground rice. Mix to a firm dough, then turn onto a floured surface and knead lightly. Divide in half and roll each piece into a 20 cm/8 inch circle. Place on greased baking sheets or in two 20 cm/8 inch round sandwich tins and prick all over with a fork. Bake for 25 minutes, or until crisp and light golden brown. Leave on the baking sheets for 5 minutes, then carefully transfer to a wire rack.

Cut one of the circles into 8 sections while still warm. Leave to cool.

Meanwhile, wash and hull the strawberries, and halve or quarter any larger ones, so that they are all the same size. Sprinkle with the caster sugar and leave on one side. Whip the cream until it stands in stiff peaks.

Just before you want to serve the shortbread, place the whole round of shortbread on a serving plate and spoon half the cream on top. Put strawberry mixture on top of that, in the centre, then spoon or pipe the rest of the cream on top in 8 heaps or whirls, spaced evenly apart around the edge of the shortcake. Then place the shortcake sections on top, arranging them at an angle, so that the cream shows underneath.

Quick Lemon Cheesecake

This is a quick and easy cheesecake which doesn't need cooking, but does need to be chilled thoroughly before it is served.

Serves 8–10

125 g (4 oz) wheatmeal biscuits
50 g (2 oz) butter
700 g (1½lb) cream cheese
grated rind and juice of 2 lemons
125 g (4 oz) caster sugar
3–4 tablespoons lemon curd (optional)

Crush the biscuits to fine crumbs with a rolling pin. Melt the butter gently in a pan, then stir in the biscuit crumbs and mix well. Press the mixture into a lightly oiled 20 cm/ 8 inch flan tin or cake tin with a loose base and put it in the fridge to chill while you make the filling.

To make the filling, beat the cream cheese until creamy, then stir in the lemon rind and juice and the caster sugar and beat again. Spoon the mixture on top of the crumb mixture in the tin. Cover with foil and chill thoroughly.

Just before serving, if you're using the lemon curd, warm this gently to soften it, then pour it on top of the cheesecake and spread to the edges. Remove the cheesecake from its tin and serve.

Quick Ice Cream

A particularly smooth ice cream, which is quick to prepare.
It is a little on the sweet side, but nevertheless liked by everyone
who tries it.

Serves 8

600 ml (1 pint) whipping cream
400 g (14 oz) can condensed skimmed milk
1 teaspoon vanilla extract

Whip the cream until thick, then add the condensed milk
and vanilla and whip again until thoroughly blended. Pour
the mixture into a polythene container and freeze until firm.

Fruit Ice Cream

Serves 6

450 g (1 lb) fresh raspberries, washed, or frozen raspberries,
   thawed
225 g (8 oz) caster sugar
600 ml (1 pint) whipping cream

Purée the raspberries in a blender or food processor, then
sieve to remove the pips. Stir in the sugar. Whip the cream
until thick, then gently fold in the raspberry purée. Pour the
mixture into a polythene container. Freeze until half solid,
then beat well and return it to the freezer until firm. Transfer
the ice cream from the freezer to the fridge 30–40 minutes
before you want to serve it.

Date, Honey and Walnut Ice Cream ♀

A delicious ice cream which is quick and easy to prepare.

Serves 6

300 ml (10 fl oz) double cream
300 ml (10 fl oz) single cream
50 g (2 oz) soft brown sugar
4 tablespoons clear honey
175 g (6 oz) pitted dates, chopped
100 g (4 oz) walnuts, chopped

Whip the double cream until it is beginning to thicken and form peaks, then add the single cream and whip again until thick. Gently stir in the sugar, honey, dates and walnuts, making sure they are all evenly distributed. Transfer the mixture to a polythene container and freeze until firm. Remove from the freezer about half an hour before you want to eat the ice cream.

Passion Fruit Sorbet ♀

Serves 4-6

600 ml (1 pint) water
225 g (8 oz) caster sugar
6–8 passion fruits
4 tablespoons lemon juice
2 egg whites

Put the water and sugar in a small heavy-based pan. Heat gently until the sugar has dissolved, then boil, uncovered, for 5 minutes. While this is happening, cut the passion fruits in half and scoop all the pulp and pips into a bowl. Remove the sugar mixture from the heat and add the passion fruit, together with the lemon juice. Cool, then freeze.

When the mixture has half frozen, whisk the egg white until beginning to peak, then gradually beat in the half-frozen mixture. Return the mixture to the freezer, and freeze until firm. Remove from the freezer 30–40 minutes before serving.

Pavlova ♀

A spectacular pudding that is always popular, yet very easy to make.

Serves 8

4 egg whites
a pinch of cream of tartar
225 g (8 oz) caster sugar
2 teaspoons white wine vinegar
4 teaspoons cornflour

For the filling

300 ml (10 fl oz) double cream
350 g (12 oz) strawberries or raspberries
a little icing sugar
Large baking sheet lined with a piece of non-stick baking parchment

Set the oven to 140°C/275°F/Gas Mark 1.

Put the egg whites and cream of tartar into a large, grease-free bowl and whisk until the egg whites are so stiff that you can turn the bowl upside down without the egg whites falling out, but don't beat them so much that the mixture starts to break up. Then add the sugar, a quarter at a time, whisking well after each addition. Mix in the vinegar and cornflour, then pipe or spoon the mixture onto the baking sheet, in a large circle, heaping it up, or piping rosettes around the edge. Bake in the oven for 1¼ hours, or until crisp and dry. Then turn off the oven and if possible leave the pavlova to cool in the oven. Strip off the paper.

Just before you are ready to serve the pavlova, whip the cream, and pile it into the centre of the ring. Arrange the fruit on top, and sift a little icing sugar over.

HOT PUDDINGS

These are lovely, warming traditional puddings, up-dated and vegetarianized by the use of wholewheat flour and vegetable suet. Most of them take a little effort to make, although there are some quick ones, such as Baked Apples, Pancakes and Traditional Rice Pudding, but they are all great when you want comforting, filling food.

Baked Apples

Serves 4

4 large cooking apples
125 g (4 oz) raisins, or
50 g (2 oz) butter or margarine
   and 50 g (2 oz) brown sugar

Preheat the oven to 180°C/350°F/Gas Mark 4.

Wash the apples, then remove the cores, using an apple corer or a sharp knife to make a neat cavity. Score the skin around the middle of each apple, then place them in an ovenproof dish. Fill the centre of the apples with the raisins, pushing them in firmly, or blend together the butter and sugar and then stuff the apples with this. Bake for about 30 minutes, or until the apples are tender when pierced with the point of a sharp knife.

Pancakes ◑

A lovely informal pudding for a chilly winter's evening, when you are eating in the kitchen and everyone can have a pancake as soon as it's ready, straight out of the pan.

Serves 4

100 g (4 oz) plain 85% wholewheat flour
½ teaspoon salt
2 eggs
150 ml (5 fl oz) milk
150 ml (5 fl oz) water
1–2 tablespoons melted butter or sunflower oil

To serve
caster sugar
1 lemon, sliced

Put all the pancake ingredients into a blender or food processor and whizz until smooth. Or put the flour and salt into a mixing bowl, mix in the beaten eggs, then gradually beat in the milk and water and melted butter.

Brush the inside of a small non-stick frying pan with oil or melted butter. Set the frying pan over a high heat until a drop of water flicked into it sizzles immediately. Remove from the heat, pour in 1½–2 tablespoons of batter for thin pancakes, more for thick ones, tipping the frying pan as you pour it in, so that the batter runs all over the bottom of the frying pan. Immediately return the pan to the heat and cook the pancake for about 30 seconds, until it is set on top and golden brown underneath, then flip the pancake over, using your fingers and a small palette knife, and cook the other side until golden brown.

Serve immediately, or stack the pancakes on a plate and keep them warm until they are all ready. Re-grease the frying pan as necessary. Serve sprinkled with sugar, with the lemon slices to squeeze over.

✳ Interleave the pancakes with squares of greaseproof paper, wrap and freeze. Reheat, covered, in a warm oven.

Rhubarb Crumble

This is easy to make because you don't need to cook the rhubarb first, and it makes a lovely spring pudding. This recipe makes a lot, but there's never any over!

Serves 4–6

900 g (2 lb) rhubarb cut into 2.5 cm/1 inch lengths
75 g (3 oz) sugar

For the crumble

250 g (9 oz) self raising 85% or 100% wholewheat flour
175 g (6 oz) butter or margarine
175 g (6 oz) demerara sugar

Preheat the oven to 200°C/400°F/Gas Mark 6.

Put the fruit in a lightly greased large shallow ovenproof dish. Mix in the sugar; make sure the fruit is in an even layer.

Put the flour in a mixing bowl and rub in the butter or margarine with your finger tips until the mixture looks like fine breadcrumbs and there are no lumps of fat showing. Add the sugar and mix gently. Spoon the crumble topping over the fruit in an even layer, covering all the fruit.

Bake for 30–40 minutes, until the crumble is crisp and lightly browned and the fruit feels tender when pierced with a skewer. Serve hot.

Apple Flan ♀

Serves 4-6

450–700 g (1–1½ lb) apples
3 heaped tablespoons apricot jam

For the pastry

175 g (6 oz) plain wholewheat flour, or half wholewheat and
    half white flour
pinch of salt
75 g (3 oz) butter or white vegetable fat, or a mixture of
    the two
2 tablespoons cold water
20–23 cm/8–9 inch flan tin or ovenproof dish

First, set the oven to 200°C/400°F/Gas Mark 6, then make
the pastry. Put the flour into a bowl with the salt. Cut the
butter and/or vegetable fat into small pieces, then rub these
into the flour with your finger tips, until the mixture looks
like breadcrumbs. Then add the water and gather the mixture
together into a dough. Roll the pastry out on a lightly floured
board and use to line a 20–23 cm/8–9 inch flan tin or dish.
Trim the edges, prick the base of the pastry all over, then
bake the flan for 15–20 minutes, until set and very lightly
browned.

   While the flan case is cooking, peel and core the apples,
and slice them into neat segments. Arrange the apple segments
in circles in the flan case. Heat the apricot jam until melted,
then pour evenly over the apples. Sprinkle with a little
cinnamon, cover with a buttered paper and bake for about
30 minutes, or until the apples are tender when pierced with
a knife. Serve hot or cold.

Gooseberry Pie

Serves 4-6
700 g (1½ lb) gooseberries, topped and tailed
175 g (6 oz) caster sugar or soft light brown sugar

For the pastry
175 g (6 oz) plain wholewheat flour, or half wholewheat and half white flour
pinch of salt
75 g (3 oz) butter or white vegetable fat, or a mixture of the two
2 tablespoons cold water
milk to glaze, or soya milk for vegans
caster sugar
900 ml (1½ pint) pie dish

First, preheat the oven to 220°C/425°F/Gas Mark 7.

Next, make the pastry. Put the flour in a bowl with the salt. Cut the butter and/or vegetable fat into small pieces, then rub these into the flour with your finger tips, until the mixture looks like breadcrumbs. Then add the water and gather the mixture together into a dough. Roll the pastry out on a lightly floured board so that it is about 2.5 cm/ 1 inch bigger all round than a 900 ml (1½ pint) pie dish. Cut a 2.5 cm/1 inch wide strip from the pastry.

Brush the rim of the pie dish with water and press the pastry strip on to it. Put the gooseberries into the pie dish and sprinkle with the sugar.

Brush the pastry strip with water, then put the large piece of pastry on top, pressing it down round the edges. Trim, knock up and flute or fork the edges. Make a steam hole in the centre of the pastry.

Cut decorations from the pastry trimmings, if you like, and stick these on to the pie with water.

Brush the pastry with milk or soya milk, and sprinkle with a little caster sugar. Bake for 10 minutes, then turn down the oven to 180°C/350°F/Gas Mark 4 and bake for a further 35–40 minutes. Sprinkle with more caster sugar and serve hot or cold.

❋

Blackcurrant Pie

Serves 4-6

700 g (1½ lb) fresh or thawed frozen blackcurrants, topped and tailed

150 g (5 oz) soft brown sugar or caster sugar

For the pastry

225 g (8 oz) plain wholewheat flour, or half wholewheat and half white flour

pinch of salt

125 g (4 oz) butter or white vegetable fat, or a mixture of the two

3 tablespoons cold water

milk to glaze, or soya milk for vegans caster sugar

24 cm/9½ inch pie plate

First put the blackcurrants into a heavy-based saucepan and cook gently for 4–5 minutes, until the juices run. Drain the fruit, to remove excess juice (which can be used for another pudding, such as a jelly). Stir the sugar into the blackcurrants. Set aside to cool.

Preheat the oven to 200°C/400°F/Gas Mark 6. Grease a 24 cm/9½ inch pie plate.

Next, make the pastry. Put the flour into a bowl with the salt. Cut the butter and/or vegetable fat into small pieces, then rub these into the flour with your finger tips, until the mixture looks like breadcrumbs. Then add the water and gather the mixture together into a dough.

On a lightly floured board, roll out just over half the pastry to a round which will fit the pie plate. Transfer this to the pie plate, using the board to help. Put the fruit into the pastry-lined plate to within 1 cm/½ inch of the edge. Dampen with water. Roll out the remaining pastry and place on top of the fruit. Press the edges together, trim, knock up and flute or fork the edges. Make a steam-hole in the centre of the pastry. Cut decorations from the pastry trimmings if you like, and stick these on to the pie with water.

Brush with milk, or soya milk, sprinkle with caster sugar, and bake for 30 minutes. Serve hot or cold.

✳

Wholewheat Treacle Tart

Serves 4

For the pastry

175 g (6 oz) plain wholewheat flour, or half wholewheat and
   half white flour
pinch of salt
75 g (3 oz) butter or white vegetable fat, or a mixture of
   the two
2 tablespoons cold water

For the filling

8 rounded tablespoons golden syrup
75 g (3 oz) soft white breadcrumbs
finely grated rind and juice of ½ lemon
20–23 cm/8–9 inch flan tin or dish, greased

To make the pastry, put the flour in a bowl, add the butter
and/or vegetable fat, cut into pieces, then rub the fat into
the flour with your finger tips until the mixture looks like
fine breadcrumbs. Add the water, then press the mixture
together with your hands to form a dough.

Roll the pastry out and use to line a greased 20-23 cm/
8-9 inch tart tin. Re-roll the pastry trimmings, then cut them
into long narrow strips, to make a trellis to go over the top
of the tart. Chill the tart and the strips of pastry while you
make the filling.

Set the oven to 200°C/400°F/Gas Mark 6. Put the syrup
in a saucepan and heat gently, to melt. Then remove from
the heat and add the breadcrumbs and lemon. Mix well, then
pour into the pastry case. Arrange the strips in a trellis pattern
on top. Bake for 10 minutes, then turn the setting down to
190°C/375°F/Gas Mark 5 and bake for a further 15 minutes.
Serve warm.

Lemon Meringue Pie ♀

Serves 4-6

For the pastry

175 g (6 oz) plain wholewheat flour, or half wholewheat and half white flour

pinch of salt

75 g (3 oz) butter or white vegetable fat, or a mixture of the two

2 tablespoons cold water

For the filling

4 tablespoons cornflour	25 g (1 oz) butter
300 ml (10 fl oz) water	2 eggs, separated
175 g (6 oz) caster sugar	*20–23 cm/8–9 inch flan tin or*
grated rind and juice of	*dish, greased*
2 small lemons	

Preheat the oven to 200°C/400°F/Gas Mark 6.

Then make the pastry. Put the flour into a bowl with the salt. Cut the butter and/or vegetable fat into small pieces, then rub these into the flour with your finger tips, until the mixture looks like breadcrumbs. Then add the water and gather the mixture together into a dough. Roll the pastry out on a lightly floured board and use to line a greased 20–23 cm/8–9 inch flan dish. Trim the edges and prick the base and bake for 20 minutes.

Meanwhile, put the cornflour in a bowl and blend to a paste with a little of the water. Bring the rest of the water to the boil with 50 g (2 oz) of the sugar. Stir into the cornflour paste, then return the mixture to the pan, add the lemon juice and rind, and stir over the heat until the mixture has thickened. Remove from the heat and then stir in the butter and egg yolks. Pour into the flan case and allow to cool.

Turn the oven to 170°C/325°F/Gas Mark 3. Whisk the egg whites until stiff and dry, then whisk in the remaining sugar. Spread the meringue over the top of the lemon mixture, being sure to take it right to the edges, to prevent the meringue from going soggy.

Bake for 40–45 minutes, until lightly browned and crisp on the outside. Serve warm or cold.

Mince Pies ♀

The mincemeat for these is best if it's made 2–3 weeks or more (up to 3 months) before you need it, though I have made good mince pies with mincemeat that I've hastily put together just a few days before Christmas!

Makes 24

450 g (1 lb) mincemeat, see recipe opposite

For the pastry

225 g/8 oz plain wholewheat flour, or half wholewheat and half white flour
pinch of salt
125 g (4 oz) butter or white vegetable fat or a mixture of the two
3 tablespoons cold water
milk to glaze, or soya milk for vegans
caster sugar
Two shallow 12-tart tartlet tins; a 7.5 cm/3 inch round pastry cutter and a 6 cm/2½ inch round pastry cutter

Preheat the oven to 200°C/400°F/Gas Mark 6. Grease the tartlet tins.

Next, make the pastry. Put the flour into a bowl with the salt. Cut the butter and/or vegetable fat into small pieces, then rub these into the flour with your finger tips, until the mixture looks like breadcrumbs. Then add the water and gather the mixture together into a dough. On a lightly floured board, roll out just over half the pastry and, using a 7.5 cm/3 inch pastry cutter, cut out 24 circles. Put these into the tartlet tins, pressing them down lightly. Then re-roll the scraps of pastry with the remaining piece of pastry, and make 24 circles with a 6 cm/2½ inch cutter.

Put a heaped teaspoon of mincemeat into each of the tartlets. Brush the edges of the pastry with water, then put one of the smaller pastry circles on top of each and press down lightly. Make a steam-hole in the centre. Brush the mince pies with milk or soya milk and sprinkle with sugar. Bake for 25–30 minutes, or until golden brown.

Mincemeat ♀

This is my mother's recipe for mincemeat, and it always brings compliments.

Makes 2 kg (7 lbs)

450 g (1 lb) cooking apples
50 g (2 oz) glacé cherries
50 g (2 oz) dates
50 g (2 oz) blanched almonds
175 g (6 oz) candied peel
450 g (1 lb) vegetarian suet
450 g (1 lb) currants
450 g (1 lb) sultanas
450 g (1 lb) raisins
350 g (12 oz) dark brown molasses sugar
½ teaspoon salt
½ teaspoon nutmeg, grated from a whole nutmeg
½ teaspoon ground ginger
1 teaspoon mixed spice
2 lemons
2 tangerines
150 ml (5 fl oz) cheapest rum or brandy

Sterilize some clean jars (enough for 2 kg/7 lb mincemeat) by heating them in a warm oven, 150°C/300°F/Gas Mark 2, for about 30 minutes.

Peel, core and grate or finely chop the apples; halve the cherries; chop the dates, almonds, and candied peel, if you're using whole candied peel (which is nicest if you can get it). Grate the vegetarian suet coarsely. Put these ingredients into a large bowl, together with the rest of the dried fruit, the sugar, salt and spices. Grate in the rind of 1 lemon and 1 tangerine, then add the juice of 2 lemons and 2 tangerines. Add the rum or brandy, then mix everything together very thoroughly with a wooden spoon. Put into the sterilized jars, cover and store in a cool, dry place.

Steamed Syrup Pudding ♀

Everyone's favourite for a chilly winter's day.

Serves 4

2 tablespoons golden syrup
125 g (4 oz) self-raising wholewheat flour, 85% or 100%
1 teaspoon baking powder
125 g (4 oz) caster sugar
125 g (4 oz) softened butter
2 eggs
warmed golden syrup for serving
900 ml (1½ pint) pudding basin

Fill a steamer with water and put on the stove to heat; or fill a saucepan with water to come half way up the 900 ml (1½ pint) pudding basin and bring the water to the boil. Meanwhile, grease the basin thoroughly with butter, then put the 2 tablespoons golden syrup in the basin.

Put the flour in a bowl with the baking powder, caster sugar, butter and eggs. Beat together with a wooden spoon for 2–3 minutes, until smooth and glossy, then spoon the mixture into the bowl on top of the syrup. Cover with a piece of greaseproof paper with a pleat in the middle (so that it can expand as the pudding rises) and a piece of foil, also pleated, and tie securely with string.

Put the basin in the steamer or saucepan, cover and steam gently for 1½ hours. Do not let the water go off the boil during this time, and keep an eye on the level of the water, topping it up with boiling water from the kettle if necessary. When it's cooked, turn the pudding out of the basin and serve with extra syrup.

Christmas Pudding ♀

Serves 8

225 g (8 oz) currants
125 g (4 oz) sultanas
125 g (4 oz) raisins
125 g (4 oz) candied peel, the whole kind, chopped, if possible
25 g (1 oz) blanched almonds, chopped
125 g (4 oz) plain flour
½ teaspoon salt
½ teaspoon nutmeg, grated from a whole nutmeg
½ teaspoon ground ginger
1½ teaspoons mixed spice
225 g (8 oz) dark brown molasses sugar
125 g (4 oz) soft wholewheat breadcrumbs
225 g (8 oz) vegetarian suet, coarsely grated
grated rind and juice of 1 lemon
2 eggs
1 tablespoon black treacle
about 4 tablespoons rum
one 1.2 litre (2 pint) pudding basin, or two 600 ml (1 pint)
pudding basins, well greased

Put the dried fruit and almonds into a large bowl; add the flour, salt, spices, sugar, breadcrumbs, vegetarian suet, lemon rind and juice, and mix well. Beat the eggs, then stir into the mixture, together with the treacle and rum. Mix well, to make a soft mixture which will fall heavily from the spoon when shaken. Spoon the mixture into the basin or basins. Cover with a double layer of greased foil, tie down well. Put into a steamer, or into a saucepan, on top of an upturned saucer, and pour round boiling water to come half way up the sides of the basin. Steam for 4 hours, topping up the water with boiling water from the kettle as necessary. Store in a cool, dry place — the pudding or puddings will keep (and mature) for several months. Steam for another 3 hours before serving.

Brandy Butter ♀ ◕

Serves 6

100 g (4 oz) unsalted butter, or unsalted margarine (from
  health food shop) for a vegan version
100 g (4 oz) soft light brown sugar or icing sugar
2 tablespoons brandy

Put the butter or margarine in a bowl and beat until light
and fluffy, then add the sugar or icing sugar and beat again.
Add the brandy, mix well. Spoon the mixture into a small
dish and chill until needed.

Rice Pudding

An old-fashioned rice pudding is cheap, easy to make,
nourishing and comforting. It is very quickly prepared but
needs to be baked for about 2 hours.

Serves 4

15 g (½ oz) butter
50 g (2 oz) short grain 'pudding' rice
2 tablespoons soft brown sugar
600 ml (1 pint) milk
fresh grated nutmeg

Set the oven to 150°C/300°F/Gas Mark 2.
  Grease a shallow casserole dish generously with half the
butter. Wash the rice in cold water, then put it in the pie
dish and add the sugar and milk. Grate some nutmeg over
the top, dot with the remaining butter, then bake for about
2 hours, until the pudding is thick and creamy, with a skin
on top. Stir the pudding after about the first 30 minutes.

9. Baking

Wholewheat flour, and, dare I say it, rather heavy, self-righteously healthy, cakes and biscuits, have long been associated with vegetarian cooking. Actually, wholewheat flour and vegetarianism aren't inseparable: you can be a meat-eating wholefood cook, using wholewheat flour, just as you can be a white-flour vegetarian.

I find I go through phases, sometimes being more wholefoody than other times, but in general I find I certainly prefer the flavour and wholesome appearance of wholewheat pastry, bread, fruit cake, gingerbread and some cookies. For some cakes and biscuits, which are essentially feather-light and delicately flavoured, I prefer white flour and choose an unbleached one for these occasional treats.

Much the same applies to sugar. We all know that too much is to be avoided, but I prefer to have the occasional cake or biscuit, perfectly made with the right proportion of sugar, rather than more frequent but less sweet and well-made goodies. Sometimes I use white sugar and sometimes real brown, depending on what is suitable for the recipe. The fat which I prefer to use for most baking is butter, although you can always use margarine instead and, if you do, I think it is worth paying a little more for one which is 'high in polyunsaturates'.

BREAD AND SCONES

Bread

Quick and Easy Wholewheat Bread

This makes a high, domed loaf with a close texture. It is quick to prepare as the dough is kneaded just once, briefly, then put straight into the tin to rise.

Makes one 450 g (1 lb) loaf

2 teaspoons dried yeast or easy-blend yeast
325 ml (8–10 fl oz) tepid water
1 teaspoon sugar
450 g (1 lb) 100% wholewheat flour, or 350 g (12 oz) wholewheat flour and 100 g (4 oz) unbleached white flour mixed
2 teaspoons salt
extra wholewheat flour
450 g (1 lb) loaf tin, well-greased

If you are using ordinary dried yeast, put it in a small jug with half the water and half the sugar, stir, then leave for 10 minutes until it's frothed up like a glass of beer. (If it doesn't froth up, it means either the yeast is stale, or that the water was too hot and has killed it; in either case, throw it away and start again, making sure the yeast is fresh.)

Put the flour in a bowl with the remaining sugar, or the whole teaspoonful, if you're using easy-blend yeast, and the salt. Stir in the easy-blend yeast, if that's what you're using, and all the tepid water. Or, if you are using dried yeast, add the frothed-up mixture to the flour, together with the remaining tepid water.

Mix to a dough, then turn the dough out onto a clean work surface and knead for 10 minutes, until the dough is smooth and silky. Flatten the dough into a rectangle and roll it up loosely to fit the tin. Put the roll into the tin with the seam underneath. Push it down into the sides and corners to give a nice domed shape to the loaf. Cover with a clean tea-towel wrung out in hot water and put in a warm place for about 30 minutes to rise.

Preheat the oven to 180°C/350°F/Gas Mark 4. When the dough has doubled in size and comes right up out of the tin, sprinkle with a little flour and bake for 40–45 minutes. Turn the loaf out of the tin. It should sound hollow when you bang it on the base. Cool on a wire rack.

The Grant Loaf

This loaf, invented by my friend, Doris Grant, has its own charm, with its moist consistency and special texture, which is full of little holes. It's a deliciously 'heavy' wholewheat bread which has become a classic, and is the easiest bread of all to make and is quickly prepared.

Makes two 450 g (1 lb) loaves

2 teaspoons dried yeast or easy-blend yeast
350 ml (12 fl oz) tepid water
1 teaspoon sugar
450 g (1 lb) 100% wholewheat flour
2 teaspoons salt
extra wholewheat flour
two 450 g (1 lb) loaf tins, well-greased

If you are using ordinary dried yeast, put it in a small jug with half the water and half the sugar, stir, then leave for 10 minutes until it's frothed up like a glass of beer. (If it doesn't froth up, it means either the yeast is stale, or that the water was too hot and has killed it. In this case, throw it away and start again, making sure the yeast is fresh.)

Put the flour in a bowl with the remaining sugar, or the whole teaspoonful, if you're using easy-blend yeast, and the salt. Stir in the easy-blend yeast, if that's what you're using, and all the tepid water. Or, if you are using dried yeast, add the frothed-up mixture to the flour, together with the remaining tepid water. Mix to a soft consistency, just too wet to knead, and then divide the dough between the two tins. Cover with a damp cloth and leave in a warm place for about 30 minutes to rise.

Meanwhile, preheat the oven to 200°C/400°F/Gas Mark 6. When the dough has risen to within 5mm/¼ inch of the tops of the tins, put them in the oven and bake for 30 minutes. Turn the loaves out on to a wire rack to cool.

Quick Baking Powder Loaf ◑

This is a quickly made emergency loaf. It's delicious when eaten warm, but stales quickly, although it can be toasted the next day.

Makes one loaf

225 g (8 oz) plain 100% wholewheat flour
½ teaspoon salt
4 teaspoons baking powder
150 ml (5 fl oz) plus 2 tablespoons milk, or soya milk for vegans
extra milk or soya milk to glaze

Preheat the oven to 220°C/425°F/Gas Mark 7.
Sift the flour, salt and baking powder together in a large bowl. Add the milk and mix quickly to a soft dough. Turn out on to a floured board and knead lightly for a minute or two until the dough is smooth. Shape into a round with your hands and place on a floured baking sheet. Brush the top with the extra milk to give a nice golden brown crust, then bake for 25–30 minutes.

Scones

Scone Ring ◑

This is a delicious and unusual scone recipe, given to me by a Scottish friend.

Makes 8 pieces

1 dessertspoon fine oatmeal
125 g (4 oz) plain wholewheat flour
2 teaspoons baking powder
25 g (1 oz) brown sugar
pinch of salt
25 g (1 oz) butter or margarine
25 g (1 oz) sultanas
6 tablespoons milk, or soya milk, for a vegan version

Set the oven to 180°C/350°F/Gas Mark 4.
   Sift together the oatmeal, flour and baking powder. Add the sugar and salt, then rub in the fat until the mixture resembles breadcrumbs. Mix to a soft pliable consistency with the milk or soya milk. Shape into a round on a floured baking tin and cut across into 8 sections. Bake for 15 minutes.

VARIATION

Treacle Scones

Use 1 tablespoon black treacle and only 4 tablespoons milk, blending the milk with the treacle before adding.

Plain Wholewheat Scones

Makes 8

225g (8 oz) self-raising wholewheat flour
½ teaspoon baking powder
50 g (2 oz) butter
2 tablespoons caster sugar
150 ml (5 fl oz) milk, approximately
milk to glaze

Sift the flour and baking powder into a bowl. Rub in the fat until the mixture resembles breadcrumbs. Stir in the sugar and add enough milk to mix to a soft dough. Turn onto a floured surface, knead lightly and roll out to a 2 cm/ ¾ inch thickness. Cut into 5 cm/2 inch rounds and place on a lightly floured baking sheet. Brush with milk and bake in a preheated oven, 220°C/425°F/Gas Mark 7, for 10 minutes. Cool on a wire rack.

Cheese-Crusted Scones

Omit the caster sugar. Add 75 g (3 oz) grated strong Cheddar cheese to the mixture before you add the milk. Roll out the dough and cut out the scones as described above, then brush them with milk and sprinkle another 25 g (1 oz) grated cheese on top. Bake as described.

CAKES

Christmas Cake ♀

Makes one 20cm (8 inch) round cake

40 g (1½ oz) whole almonds
175 g (6 oz) plain wholewheat flour
1 teaspoon mixed spice
175 g (6 oz) butter
175 g (6 oz) brown sugar
5 eggs
1 tablespoon black treacle
250 g (9 oz) currants
175 g (6 oz) sultanas
175 g (6 oz) raisins
75 g (3 oz) whole candied peel, chopped
50 g (2 oz) glacé cherries, rinsed under hot water, dried and halved
75 g (3 oz) ground almonds
grated rind and juice of 1 lemon
1 tablespoon brandy
20 cm/8 inch round cake tin

Put the almonds in a small saucepan, cover with cold water and bring to the boil. Then drain, slip off the skins, and chop the nuts.

Preheat the oven to 150°C/300°F/Gas Mark 2. Grease a 20 cm/8 inch round cake tin, line with 3 layers of greased greaseproof paper, and tie a piece of brown paper around the outside, so that it extends 5 cm/2 inches above the top of the tin.

Sift the flour and mixed spice into a basin, mixing in any bran left in the sieve. Beat the butter and sugar in a bowl until light and fluffy. Beat the eggs, then add to the creamed butter mixture a teaspoonful at a time, beating well after each addition. Add the treacle, then fold in the flour, followed by all the remaining ingredients except the brandy. Spoon the mixture into the prepared tin, making a slight depression in the centre, so that when the cake rises it will be level, rather than domed in the middle. Bake for $4\frac{1}{2}$–5 hours, or until a warmed knife inserted in the centre comes out clean. If the cake needs more baking, put it back in the oven, but watch it carefully.

Cool the cake for 30 minutes in the tin, then turn the cake out on to a wire rack to finish cooling. When it's cold, peel off the paper. Prick the cake all over with a skewer, cocktail stick or fine knitting needle and pour the brandy over. Wrap the cake in two layers of greaseproof paper and store in an airtight tin until ready for icing.

ICING THE CHRISTMAS CAKE

3–4 heaped tablespoons redcurrant jelly
1 portion almond paste (page 174)
1 portion mouldable icing (page 175)
few drops food colouring for decoration

Before icing the cake, trim the top of the cake level if necessary, so that you have a flat surface to work on.

Heat the redcurrant jelly in a saucepan until melted, then brush this all over the top and sides of the cake.

Roll out half the almond paste into a circle 1 cm/$\frac{1}{2}$inch bigger all round than the cake and a thickness of 1 cm/$\frac{1}{2}$ inch. Press this lightly on top of the cake and trim the edges level with the sides of the cake.

Measure round the circumference of the cake with a piece of string, and use another piece to measure the depth of the cake. Roll out the remaining almond paste into a long strip the length and depth measured by the pieces of string. Gently press this strip round the sides of the cake. Put the cake on a cake board.

Next, roll the icing out thinly to a circle large enough to cover the top and sides of the cake. Carefully lift the icing up and place on top of the cake, gently pressing it into position. Trim off the excess. Colour the remaining icing and cut into decorations, using a knife or small pastry cutters.

Almond Paste

Enough to cover the top and sides of a 20 cm/8 inch cake.

350 g (12 oz) ground almonds
175 g (6 oz) caster sugar
175 g (6 oz) icing sugar
2 teaspoons lemon juice
2–3 drops almond essence
1 egg, beaten
a little cornflour

Put the almonds in a bowl with the caster sugar and icing sugar. Make a well in the centre and add the lemon juice, almond essence and a little of the beaten egg. Mix gently, adding enough beaten egg to make a firm paste. Turn the mixture out on to a board or working surface sprinkled with cornflour and knead lightly, but don't over-knead it, or the almond paste will become oily. Store the almond paste in a polythene bag until needed; it will keep for 2–3 weeks.

Mouldable Icing ♀

This is a useful icing that you roll out to use; and the trimmings can be cut into shapes to make decorations for the cake. This recipe makes enough to cover a 20 cm/8 inch cake with some over to make decorations.

50 g (2 oz) unsalted butter or margarine
4 tablespoons lemon juice
about 700 g (1½ lb) icing sugar

Put the butter or margarine in a large saucepan with the lemon juice and melt gently. Add about a third of the icing sugar, mix well, and heat gradually to simmering point. Let the mixture simmer gently for 2 minutes, then remove from the heat and add half of the rest of the icing sugar, mixing well. Then gradually add enough of the remaining sugar to make a soft, mouldable consistency, like a warm well-worked plasticine. Turn out on to a surface that's been lightly sprinkled with icing sugar and knead gently until smooth and glossy. Store in a polythene bag until needed; it will keep satisfactorily, well-wrapped, in the fridge for at least a month.

Wholewheat Dundee Cake

300 g (10 oz) plain 100% wholewheat flour
2 teaspoons baking powder
175 g (6 oz) butter
175 g (6 oz) brown sugar
3 eggs, lightly beaten
225 g (8 oz) sultanas
175 g (6 oz) currants
50 g (2 oz) candied peel — whole candied peel, chopped, is nicest
50 g (2 oz) glacé cherries, rinsed under hot water, dried and halved
grated rind of 1 lemon
50 g (2 oz) ground almonds
milk, if necessary
25 g (1 oz) blanched almonds, split in half
18 cm/7 inch round cake tin

Grease the tin, then line with a double layer of greased greaseproof paper. Preheat the oven to 160°C/325°F/Gas Mark 3.

Sift the flour with the baking powder and mix in the bran which is left in the sieve. Beat the butter and sugar in a bowl until light and fluffy, then add the beaten egg, a teaspoonful at a time, beating well after each addition, to prevent curdling. If it should curdle, just add a bit of flour, then continue with the egg: the cake won't have such a perfect texture, but it will taste just as good.

When all the egg is in, fold in the flour and all the other ingredients except the split almonds. Add a tablespoonful of milk to the mixture if necessary, so that it will drop heavily from the spoon when it's tapped against the side of the basin, but don't make the mixture too soft. Spoon the mixture into the tin and make a slight depression in the top. Arrange the almonds lightly on top, without pressing them in. Bake for 2 hours, or until a warmed skewer, inserted into the centre, comes out clean.

Cool in the tin for 30 minutes, then turn out onto a wire rack to finish cooling. When the cake is quite cold, strip off the paper. Store in an airtight tin.

Quick Wholewheat Jam Sandwich Cake ♀

This sponge cake is easy to make and popular with everyone.

Makes one 20 cm/8 inch cake.

175 g (6 oz) self-raising wholewheat flour, 85% or 100%
1½ teaspoons baking powder
175 g (6 oz) caster sugar
175 g (6 oz) softened butter
3 eggs

For the filling

4 tablespoons warmed raspberry jam
a little caster sugar
two 20 cm/8 inch sandwich tins

Preheat the oven to 170°C/325°F/Gas Mark 3. Grease two 20 cm/8 inch sandwich tins and line the base of each with a circle of greased greaseproof paper.

Sift the flour with the baking powder into a mixing bowl and add the sugar, butter and eggs. Beat with a wooden spoon for 2 minutes, or in an electric mixer for about 1 minute, until the mixture is smooth, thick and glossy. Spoon the mixture into the prepared tins and level the tops.

Bake, without opening the oven door, for 30 minutes, until the cakes spring back when lightly touched in the centre. Leave the cakes in the tins to cool for 1 minute, then turn them out on to a wire rack and carefully remove the lining paper, then leave the cakes to cool completely.

Sandwich the cakes together with the warmed jam and sprinkle the top with caster sugar.

 ·

Sticky Wholewheat Gingerbread

A wonderful gingerbread (my mother's recipe) which gets stickier and stickier the longer it's kept, though, I must say, it's not too easy to keep . . .

Makes 16 pieces

50 g (2 oz) golden syrup
175 g (6 oz) black treacle
125 g (4 oz) butter or margarine
225 g (8 oz) plain wholewheat flour
2 teaspoons baking powder
½ teaspoon ground ginger
75 g (3 oz) molasses sugar
2 eggs, beaten
50 g (2 oz) chopped walnuts, candied peel or preserved ginger
— all optional
½ teaspoon bicarbonate of soda
200 ml (7 fl oz) milk
20 cm/8 inch square tin

Grease a 20 cm/8 inch square tin and line with two layers of greased greaseproof paper. Preheat the oven to 180°C/350°F/Gas Mark 4.

Put the golden syrup, treacle and butter or margarine into a pan and heat gently until melted. Cool until you can put your hand against the side of the pan.

Meanwhile, sift the flour into a bowl with the baking powder and ginger, adding also the bran left behind in the sieve. Add the sugar, and the nuts, peel or ginger if you're using them. Make a well in the centre and pour in the cooled melted ingredients and the beaten eggs. Stir the bicarbonate of soda into the milk, then quickly add to the rest of the ingredients, mixing well.

Pour the mixture into the tin. Bake in the preheated oven for 1½ hours, or until well-risen and firm to the touch. Cool for 30 minutes in the tin, then lift out on to a wire rack to finish cooling. Strip off the paper when the gingerbread is cold, and cut the gingerbread into pieces.

Rock Cakes

Makes 12

225 g (8 oz) plain wholewheat flour
2 teaspoons baking powder
1 teaspoon mixed spice
125 g (4 oz) butter or margarine
125 g (4 oz) brown sugar
125 (4 oz) mixed dried fruit
1 egg

Preheat the oven to 230°C/450°F/Gas Mark 8. Grease a baking sheet.

Sift the flour, baking powder and mixed spice into a bowl, adding also the residue of bran left in the sieve. Rub the butter or margarine into the flour with your fingers, until the mixture looks like fine breadcrumbs, then stir in the sugar and dried fruit. Beat the egg, and add to the mixture, to make a consistency that just holds together; it should be crumbly, not too soft.

Put rough heaps of mixture on to a baking sheet, allowing a little room between them for spreading. Bake for 12–15 minutes, until the cakes are lightly browned and there is no uncooked mixture in the centre. Transfer them to a wire rack to cool. Store in an airtight tin.

✳

Chocolate Crispies ◔

A popular treat for children, and they couldn't be easier to make.

Makes 16

250 g (9 oz) plain or milk chocolate
125 g (4 oz) cornflakes
16 paper cake cases

Break the chocolate into pieces and put the pieces into a large bowl. Set the bowl over a pan of gently simmering water and leave for a few minutes until the chocolate has melted, stirring from time to time. Stir in the cornflakes, so they are coated with chocolate. Spoon the mixture into the cake cases and leave to set.

BISCUITS

Rich Vanilla Biscuits ◑

Makes 15-18 rolled out into balls the size of walnuts

50 g (2 oz) butter or margarine
25 g (1 oz) white vegetable fat
40 g (1 oz) caster sugar
125 g (4 oz) plain 85% or 100% wholewheat flour
1 teaspoon baking powder
1 teaspoon vanilla essence

Preheat the oven to 180°C/350°F/Gas Mark 4.

Beat together the butter or margarine, vegetable fat and the caster sugar until light and fluffy, then add the flour, baking powder and vanilla essence, and mix to a dough. Knead lightly, then form into balls the size of a large marble, place on an ungreased baking sheet and press down with a fork to flatten. Bake for 15–20 minutes, until golden brown at the edges. Cool slightly, then transfer to a wire rack to finish cooling. Store in an airtight tin.

Chocolate Chip Cookies ◖

Makes 20

100 g (4 oz) butter
75 g (3 oz) caster sugar
50 g (2 oz) soft brown sugar
1 egg
1 teaspoon vanilla essence
150 g (5 oz) plain flour
¼ teaspoon bicarbonate of soda
½ teaspoon salt
100 g (4 oz) chocolate or carob chips

Set the oven to 190°C/375°F/Gas Mark 5. Brush several baking sheets with oil or melted vegetable fat.

Beat the butter with the caster sugar and brown sugar until light, then beat in the egg and vanilla essence. Add the flour, bicarbonate of soda and salt and mix well, then stir in the chocolate or carob chips.

Form teaspoonfuls of the mixture into balls and place on the baking sheets, leaving enough space to allow for spreading during cooking. Bake for about 10 minutes, or until lightly browned all over and deeper brown at the edges. Leave on the baking sheet for 10 minutes to cool, then lift the cookies off with a fish slice and put them onto a wire rack to finish cooling.

Shortbread

Makes 28 inch rounds

175 g (6 oz) butter
75 g (3 oz) caster sugar
175 g (6 oz) plain flour, sifted
75 g (3 oz) ground rice

Set the oven to 180°C/350°F/Gas Mark 4.

Beat the butter until soft and fluffy, then beat in the sugar. Stir in the flour until well mixed, then stir in the ground rice. Mix to a firm dough, then turn onto a floured surface and knead lightly. Divide in half and roll each piece into a 20 cm/8 inch circle. Place on greased baking sheets or into two 2 cm/8 inch round sandwich tins and prick all over with a fork. Bake for 25 minutes, or until crisp and light golden brown.

Mark into sections while still hot. Leave on the baking sheets for 5 minutes, then carefully transfer to a wire rack.

Cheese Biscuits

Makes approximately 2 dozen

175 g (6 oz) plain 100% wholewheat flour
pinch of cayenne pepper
125 g (4 oz) butter or margarine
50 g (2 oz) Cheddar cheese, grated

Preheat the oven to 150°C/300°F/Gas Mark 2. Put the flour into a bowl with the cayenne pepper and rub in the butter or margarine until the mixture looks like fine breadcrumbs. Add the cheese, then press the mixture together into a dough. Roll out the dough to a thickness of 5mm/¼ inch, cut into shapes and place them on a baking sheet. Bake for 30 minutes, or until lightly browned. Cool slightly, then transfer to a wire rack to finish cooling completely. Store in an airtight tin.

✳

10. Nutrients in the Vegetarian Diet

The main difference between the vegetarian diet and what is generally considered a normal diet is that a vegetarian diet does not contain meat or fish, that vegetable fats are used instead of animal fats (such as lard and suet), and that more wholewheat bread, fruit and vegetables are eaten.

As long as a vegetarian is eating a fairly balanced menu (see below), getting enough **protein** is not usually a problem; a meat diet in fact supplies in excess of daily needs. Dishes made from concentrated vegetarian proteins such as pulses (eg lentils, red kidney beans or butter beans), nuts and seeds, eggs or dairy produce such as milk and cheese, will supply adequate protein in the way that meat or fish dishes do. If you are worried about protein — perhaps because someone in your family needs a high-protein diet — you can add protein to many dishes by adding beaten eggs to sauces or to mashed potatoes, for instance, fortifying milk by whisking in some powdered milk, by stirring soya flour into gravies or adding a little to savoury bakes as well as bread, biscuits and cakes. Peanuts, peanut butter, sesame seeds and spread, wheatgerm, soya beans and soya products and cheese are other vegetarian foods which are particularly high in protein.

The vegetarian diet usually supplies plenty of **Vitamin C**, because plenty of fresh fruits and vegetables are generally included, and these are good sources. But if you're concerned about this vitamin (perhaps in the diet of a fussy child), good concentrated sources, apart from blackcurrants, are green and red peppers, kiwi fruits, strawberries, oranges and tangerines.

Vitamin A, found in dairy produce and in green vegetables and yellow-orange fruits and vegetables, is also usually well-supplied, although vegans need to make sure that they are including enough non-dairy sources. Carrots, red peppers, dark green leafy vegetables such as spinach are rich in Vitamin

A, as are apricots (both dried and fresh), peaches and cantaloupe melon, which is particularly rich.

The **B vitamins** need particular attention in a vegetarian diet. But there shouldn't be a deficit as long as you are eating wholegrain cereals, wholewheat bread, some nuts and pulses, fresh fruit and vegetables, and yeast extracts, which contain B vitamins and are also fortified with extras. Brewer's yeast is a particularly rich source of B vitamins, and you can take some of this each day, either in powder form, sprinkled over fruit juice or breakfast cereal for instance, or in the form of yeast tablets, which you can get at the chemist or health shop. Other foods which are particularly good sources of B vitamins are wheatgerm, black-eyed beans, soya beans and soya products, avocados, peas and beans, endive, mushrooms, dried fruit, eggs, almonds, peanuts, sunflower and sesame seeds, bananas, dark green leafy vegetables, and the seaweeds nori and hiziki.

Folic acid and B12 are two of the B vitamin group which need care, especially if no dairy produce is eaten, and, to be on the safe side, I think it does no harm to take a vitamin tablet containing these.

Vitamin D is not found in many foods. The main sources are oily fish (obviously not applicable to vegetarians and vegans), eggs and fortified margarine. I think it's wise to take a vitamin tablet containing this vitamin to be on the safe side.

To sum up, both a vegetarian diet and a vegan diet can supply all the vitamins and minerals needed for health (and a good vegetarian diet supplies a super-abundance of some of them as well as enzymes, the role of which is less well-known). However, it may be advisable to top up the diet with a good multi-vitamin tablet. Choose a vitamin tablet containing vitamin D and also folic acid if possible: this is included in some effervescent vitamin tablets now available.

Iron is another nutrient which can cause concern to vegetarians and vegans, although there are some good sources of this mineral available. These include lentils, the ubiquitous but rather unpalatable soya bean and its products, dried fruits, especially apricots and peaches, dates, figs, also prunes and prune juice (which is fairly palatable taken with a shot of soda), whole grains, especially millet, and wheatgerm, broccoli and all dark green leafy vegetables; nuts, especially pistachios, almonds and cashews; and sunflower and sesame seeds, and, particularly, pumpkin seeds; egg yolk, molasses, black treacle, unrefined dark molasses sugar, carob and chocolate. All the edible seaweeds are good sources, but especially hiziki.

Getting enough **calcium** isn't usually a problem for vegetarians who are eating dairy produce. For vegans, it is important to include several servings each day of other calcium-rich foods such as dried figs, broccoli, soya beans and soya products, almonds, brazil nuts, sunflower seeds, sesame seeds and sesame cream and edible seaweeds, particularly hiziki.

PLANNING A DAY'S MEALS

The main guidelines when planning healthy meals are to include as much fresh foods as possible — particularly fruit and vegetables, grains and pulses — and to keep a check on the levels of fat and sugar. It's also important that you choose foods you like and that meal-times should be a pleasure.

Some people become vegetarian literally overnight; others make the decision, and then put it into practice gradually, replacing one meal after another, week by week, with a vegetarian one. People usually find it easiest to make meals similar to the ones they've been used to, but with vegetarian main dishes instead of meat ones.

Breakfasts

Breakfast is an easy meal to vegetarianize; for many people, weekday breakfasts are vegetarian in any case, but some simple vegetarian cooked breakfasts would be poached, scrambled or boiled eggs; cheese and tomatoes on toast; mushrooms or baked beans on toast; cheesey tomatoes (page 13); a jacket potato (quick and easy if you have a microwave oven) or, for a special cooked breakfast, fried onions, tomatoes, mushrooms and potatoes with fried bread and perhaps Hazel Nut and Vegetable Burgers (page 79), or Chestnut Sausages (page 81), or Spanish Omelette (page 83).

Lunches

There are ideas for quick and simple vegetarian lunches in the snack section of this book; Sandwiches (page 19), Toasted Sandwiches (page 16), Filled Pitta Bread (page 17), Filled French Bread (page 18), or Vegetarian Burger Buns (page 15), are all good. Or an Omelette (page 12), Blue Cheese Dip (page 13), or Avocado Dip (page 29), with Crudités (page 28), or Hummus (page 27), with pitta bread; or a bowl of quickly made homemade soup such as Lentil (page 23), Tomato (page 22), or Leek and Potato (page 24). A Baked Potato (page 10), makes a good, filling lunch, especially if served with some salad; or Bulgar Wheat Salad (page 118) which is a meal in itself, as is Colourful Bean Salad (page 119) served in pitta pockets, or Vitality Salad (page 116).

Main Meals

Main vegetarian meals can be planned on the 'meat and two veg' theme, with a meatless savoury as the main dish. There are many possibilities, such as Vegetable Crumble (page 66), Stuffed Peppers (page 71), Nut Roast (page 75), Hazel Nut and Vegetable Burgers (page 79), Savoury Mushroom, Nut and Tomato Bake (page 74), Lentil Roast (page 41), Cheese and Onion Roll (page 98), Savoury Vegetable Pudding (page 102), or Wholewheat Vegetable Pie (page 104). Some of these are enhanced with a sauce: Tomato Sauce (page 136), goes well with Stuffed Peppers, and Vegetarian Gravy is good with the nut dishes, Lentil Roast, Cheese and Onion Roll and Savoury Pudding. Some dishes are pretty well complete in themselves: Vegetable Casserole (page 72), Easy Lentil Stew (page 37), and Vegetable Curry with Brown Rice (page 46), for instance; others only need a crisp salad to go with them; Pizza (page 90), Paella (page 50), Risotto (page 52), Rigatoni with Tomato Sauce (page 57), Potato Bake (page 65), Creamy Macaroni Bake (page 59). Cheese Fritters (page 89) are good served with chips or new potatoes, a vegetable, such as green beans, and parsley sauce.

Some of the dishes in this book are very quick and easy to make, which is particularly valuable if there's only one vegetarian in the family. In this case, a freezer can also be invaluable, because you can make up a full quantity of a recipe then freeze portions which the vegetarian can eat when meat is on the menu for the rest of the family. A friend of mine always keeps a stock of Spiced Vegetable Pasties (page 99) in the freezer.

One of the challenges which beginner-cooks face, whether they're vegetarian or not, is co-ordinating the preparation of the meal so that everything is done at the same time. This gets easy with experience, but in the early days it's helpful to make a main dish which can be fully prepared in advance ready for cooking, so that you can then concentrate on the vegetables. Timings for vegetables are given in the vegetable section of this book. Alternatively, you could serve the main dish with a salad, which is often the most pleasant accompaniment.

Special Meals

When you're making a vegetarian meal, or entertaining vegetarian friends, planning is easier if you first decide on the main course and then select a starter and dessert which complement it. If possible, avoid choosing two dishes which contain the same ingredient in any quantity (such as garlic mushrooms followed by mushroom flan), or which are the same colour (tsatsiki to start with, vanilla ice cream for pudding), or of the same shape (a big round pizza followed by a big round pavlova), or which are very creamy or rich (pears with tarragon cream, followed by mushrooms in cream on brown rice, followed by nectarines with creamy topping . . .). But don't worry too much; choose recipes you like making and eating, do as much advance preparation as you can, then enjoy yourself. Here are some menu suggestions:

Tsatsiki (page 30) with Crudités (page 28)
Spiced Vegetables and Saffron rice (page 48)
with Dal (page 40)
Exotic Fruit Salad (page 141)

*

Cucumber, Radish and Hiziki Salad (page 115)
Mushrooms in Cream Sauce with Brown Rice (page 53)
Broccoli (page 123) or Spinach (page 129)
Dried Fruit Compote (page 143)

*

Tomato Soup (page 22)
Fettucine with Cream and Blue Cheese (page 55)
Green Salad (page 113)
Pears in Red Wine (page 142)

*

Vegetables à la Grecque (page 33)

Vegetarian Lasagne al Forno (page 60)
French beans (page 125)
Nectarines with Cream Topping (page 145)

*

Hummus (page 27) with warm pitta bread
Stir-Fried Vegetables (page 63)
Mashed potatoes (page 127) or Brown Rice (page 46)
Green Salad (page 113)
Date, Walnut and Honey Ice Cream (page 150)

*

Avocado Dip (page 29) with Crudités (page 28)
Aubergrine Bake (page 67)
New potatoes
Green Salad (page 113)
Peaches in Wine (page 142)

*

Lentil Soup (page 23)
Asparagus Triangles (page 100)
Soured Cream Sauce (page 138)
Carrots (page 123) and Broccoli (page 123)
Fruit Ice Cream (page 149)

*

For Christmas:
Pears with Tarragon Cream (page 31)
White Nut Roast with Herb Stuffing (page 77)
Gravy (page 135), Bread Sauce (page 138), Cranberry Sauce
(page 137)
Roast Potatoes (page 127)
Brussel Sprouts, Carrots
Christmas Pudding and Brandy Butter (page 163 and 164)

11. Using the Freezer

Many vegetarian dishes freeze well and in this book those which do are marked (F). In general, make sure all food is thoroughly cold before putting it into the freezer, then pack it well and label it clearly. I find it helpful to add any relevant comments to the label, such as 'Delicious', or 'add 1 crushed garlic clove before using'. Sometimes it's most convenient to cut a savoury, such as a nut roast, into slices before freezing, so that you can later extract the correct number of portions and perhaps heat them up quickly in the microwave (see below). If you're doing this, it's best to freeze the item after cooking, rather than before.

Burgers or fritters are nicest frozen before frying; spread them out on a tray, freeze until solid, then pack. They can be shallow-fried gently in hot oil while still frozen: cook them slowly, so that the centre is cooked through by the time the outside is done.

Liquids such as soups and some sauces, such as gravy and tomato sauce, freeze well. Freeze them in useful-size portions in containers which allow some head-room for the liquid to expand as it freezes.

Bread, cakes and biscuits freeze well. To use, unwrap them and stand them on a wire rack to thaw out. Biscuits thaw very quickly, in less than 30 minutes, if spread out well.

12. Using the Microwave

A microwave oven can be used to speed up cooking processes, such as melting butter, syrup and chocolate. It can also replace the hob for some cooking processes such as frying onions; put the onions and oil into a bowl and microwave on full for a few minutes, stirring 2–3 times. Or you can make white sauce by putting all the ingredients in a jug in the microwave for 4–5 minutes, or until thickened, stirring well 2–3 times. I personally prefer to do these jobs in a saucepan in the usual way. It depends how microwave-minded you are!

But a microwave oven is invaluable for heating up portions of food (or complete dishes) from the freezer. Complete dishes are best thawed first; individual portions don't need to be.

Vegetables also cook very well in the microwave oven, and, although there's no saving in time (except with things like jacket potatoes), the flavour and texture are good because of the small amount of water used. Rice and pulses can also be cooked very cleanly in the microwave, but without any real saving in time. Rice is cooked by the absorption method (page 46), and brown rice takes 30–40 minutes on full power.

Pulses should be soaked in the usual way, and red kidney beans should be boiled hard on top of the cooker for 10 minutes before you transfer them to a casserole dish; cover generously with water, put a plate or non-metal lid over the top, and microwave for 10–15 minutes for lentils, 40–50 minutes for larger beans, or until they are tender. For further details of pulse, cereal and vegetable cookery, consult the handbook which comes with your microwave.

13. Notes on Flavourings and Ingredients

FLAVOURINGS

Black Olives/Black Olive Pâté Just a little adds a piquant, almost smoky flavour to savoury mixtures (see Spaghetti Bolognese on page 57) and is also good in sandwiches and vegetarian cocktail nibbles. Black olive pâté is available in a jar in some delicatessens and health food shops; otherwise, buy good black olives (I like Kalmati olives or giant olives, from Greece) from a delicatessen counter and stone and mash one or two to make a paste.

Chilli, Green Fresh green chilli gives a hot taste to dishes such as Dal (page 40) and Avocado Dip (page 29). Many greengrocers stock green chillies, and usually only one is needed. Halve, de-seed then finely chop the chilli, but take care not to touch your face or eyes until you've washed your hands, as the juice can be irritating.

Garlic Always useful; buy the biggest, juiciest-looking bulbs you can find. Break off the individual cloves as you need them, peel and crush on a board, holding a knife flat, or in a garlic press.

Miso A thick, sticky brown substance, rather similar in flavour and appearance to yeast extract, but made from fermented soya beans. Add to soups and stews just before serving to preserve flavour.

Salt Sea salt gives the best flavour and is the kind preferred by health experts (but in moderation!). My favourite is the flaky kind (Tidman's), which you can scrunch over food with your fingers.

Soy Sauce Useful for giving foods both a savoury flavour and an attractive brown colour. Choose a make which is made from soya beans and salt and doesn't contain caramel and other additives. Shoyu and Tamari are types of soy sauce, both excellent.

Stock Powder/Concentrate Several good vegetarian types are available, so try in small sizes to find your favourite. I like Marigold Bouillon powder and Hügli concentrate best.

Tomato Purée Useful for giving an intense tomato flavour to soups, sauces, nut roasts. I find it useful to keep a tube in the fridge.

Yeast Extract Gives a savoury taste to soups, sauces, nut roasts and gravies, or in sandwiches. Flavours vary from brand to brand, so it's worth experimenting.

SPICES

Buy small quantities of spices, as you need them, from a shop with a rapid turnover and store them in air-tight containers.

Cardamom Buy in pods and add a few to spiced vegetables and rice mixtures for a delicious eucalyptus-like flavour.

Cayenne A type of hot pimento; a pinch gives a kick to cheese dishes, but it's hot, so use with caution.

Chilli Powder The strength of this varies, so add a little at a time and taste. Used in making a Vegetarian Chilli (page 39) and for adding a bite to bean, pulse and cheese dishes.

Cinnamon Can be bought in both powder and stick form. The sticks are useful for adding to spicy mixtures, like Spiced Rice (page 48) and the powder is best for use in cakes and for sprinkling over puddings, such as the Easy Yogurt Pudding on page 144.

Cloves Both whole cloves and ground gloves are useful; whole cloves are often stuck into an onion to flavour dishes such as Bread Sauce (page 138) and Cheese Fritters (page 89).

Ground cloves are useful in baking and Red Cabbage Casserole (page 133).

Coriander, Whole and Ground Ground coriander is indispensable as a flavouring for Spiced Vegetables (page 48) and Dal (page 40). Whole coriander seeds, which are lightly crushed before use — with a teaspoon, end of a rolling pin or in a pestle and mortar — have a refreshing, burnt-orange flavour and are delicious in Vegetables à la Grecque (page 33) and Vegetable Curry (page 46).

Cumin Available both whole and ground; brings a warming flavour to curries and spicy dishes.

Curry Powder A mixture of spices; I find it useful to have a small tin of commercial curry powder on the shelf, for adding to spicy mixtures and giving a lift to nut roasts and some cheese and egg dishes.

Ginger The ginger root is available in several forms, the most useful for general cookery being fresh ginger, which you buy at the greengrocers and just wash and grate (I don't bother to peel it). Ground ginger, the dried powdered form is useful for cakes and in curries when fresh ginger isn't available. Preserved ginger — in syrup or crystallized — is a pleasant ingredient in cakes and some puddings.

Mace Available whole, in blades, or powdered. One or two blades can be added to milk to flavour it for sauces or delicate dishes (strain it off before use); or a pinch of the powder can be used for the same effect in sauces, cheese, nut and egg dishes.

Mixed Spice A commercial mix of sweet spices, including ginger, cloves, nutmeg and cinnamon, used in cakes and biscuits.

Mustard Dry mustard powder is useful for adding zip to some cheese dishes, such as Cheese Fritters (page 89) a made-up mustard in a jar is good in salad dressings. I like Grey Poupon Dijon mustard.

Nutmeg After pepper, probably the most useful spice excellent in both sweet and savoury dishes, as well as in cakes. It is always best to buy whole nutmegs and grate them as you need them, on a special small nutmeg grater or the finest holes of an ordinary grater.

Paprika Pepper The best variety of this pretty scarlet spice is Hungarian. It is mild, used in Vegetarian Chilli (page 39) and for sprinkling on top of pale savoury dishes to give them some colour.

Pepper Black peppercorns, freshly ground in a pepper mill, give the best flavour to most dishes, although I like to use white pepper (preferably freshly ground from white peppercorns in a pepper mill) occasionally for some delicate dishes. It's interesting to vary them, because the two types differ in flavour, white pepper being sweeter but less aromatic.

Saffron Used to flavour and colour a dish such as Spiced Rice. (page 48). Saffron is the stamens from a certain species of crocus, and if you buy it in the form of stamens or 'strands', rather than powdered, you can be sure it's the real thing. It is expensive, but only a little — about 6 strands — is needed for colouring and flavouring a dish of rice, for example.

Tumeric Bright yellow, with quite a strong taste. Used to colour and flavour vegetable and rice dishes such as Vegetable Curry (page 46).

Vanilla The long black pods give a subtle flavour to custards and ice creams (page 149). A vanilla pod is heated with the milk, which draws out the flavour, then rinsed, dried and used again. A vanilla pod can also be broken in half and the halves buried in a jar of caster sugar, which results in a delicately vanilla-flavoured sugar. The sugar can be topped up as it's used. Vanilla essence is useful, too; read the label and make sure you buy real vanilla essence or extract rather than the synthetic type.

HERBS

It's interesting how the flavour of dried herbs differs from its fresh counterpart. The only one which really benefits from drying is bay, in which the flavour becomes more intense. Fresh herbs generally give a better result, although you need to use three times as much to get the equivalent strength of flavour. As fresh herbs are not always easy to come by, I've assumed in the recipe that you're using dried herbs unless I specify fresh, where dried wouldn't be suitable. For buying herbs, see my comments about buying spices, as the same applies.

Basil Fresh basil is one of the most delicious summer herbs and goes particularly well with tomatoes. Dried basil is useful, too, especially in Tomato Sauce (page 136) and Vegetarian Bolognese (page 57).

Bay Good in savoury stews, gravies, to flavour white sauce and rice pudding delicately.

Bouquet Garni A bunch of herbs tied together and used in many savoury dishes, particularly stews, vegetable dishes. The mixture usually contains a bay leaf, some parsley stalks (which are full of flavour) and a sprig of thyme (which is a useful herb as it's trouble-free to grow and can survive the winter, so may be available fresh all the year). Sometimes some thin slivers of lemon rind are added, and the whole lot may be encased in a leek, slit to make a pocket, then tied up. The leek itself adds to the flavour of the bouquet garni. Remove the whole thing before serving.

Chives Only worth using fresh, I think. They make a pretty garnish and give a delicate onion flavour when snipped with scissors on top of soups, salads, dips.

Coriander The plant which bears the seeds described in the spices section. Once tasted, fresh coriander is never forgotten and is very common in Indian and Middle Eastern dishes. It is delicious chopped quite lavishly over spiced vegetables. There is no dried replacement — fresh parsley is the nearest equivalent.

197

Curry Leaves Aromatic leaves which taste spicy, like curry powder. They can be used fresh or dried and are good in spiced vegetable dishes, like the one on page 48, but use a pinch or two of curry powder instead if you can't get them.

Herbes de Provence A wonderful, aromatic mixture — the French equivalent of our mixed herbs — which somehow manages to make everything taste much more 'French'!

Marjoram A sweetly-flavoured herb with a slightly musky after-taste. Good in nut roasts, stuffings and stews. I find the dried variety as useful as the fresh.

Mint Very useful in its fresh form for all kinds of salads and cold dishes and for garnishing both sweet and savoury fruit mixtures, but I don't think dried mint is worth buying. Instead, keep a jar of mint sauce concentrate in the cupboard and use a little of that in the winter, when fresh mint is unavailable.

Mixed Herbs All-purpose mixture of herbs, generally useful in savoury dishes.

Oregano Another herb which I do not think is harmed too much by drying; oregano gives an 'Italian' flavour to pizzas and pasta dishes.

Parsley Only worth using fresh, and it can be used lavishly. The flat-leaf variety (often from Cyprus), which you can sometimes buy in big bunches, has the most intense flavour and is my favourite. Keep the stems for flavouring stews and sauces — remove them before serving.

Rosemary Another useful one which survives the winter, at least where I live. It has a pine-flavour and a little goes a long way, but it can be pleasant in vegetable casseroles and nut roasts.

Sage Perhaps this would be described as giving an 'English' flavour to stuffings and nut roasts . . . Drying does not harm it too much. Good with onions.

Tarragon Delicate and good used fresh in salads, omelettes and vegetable dishes, and snipped over soups, but I don't think dried tarragon is worth buying. A sprig of fresh tarragon in a bottle of white wine vinegar will flavour it (leave the tarragon in the bottle).

Thyme Very savoury and useful in many dishes. It over-winters well, although it survives the drying process without too much damage, too.

FATS AND OILS

Butter Gives an excellent flavour to most cooking; I use a lightly salted butter (or concentrated butter) for general use, and unsalted butter at the table and for delicate dishes.

Margarine If you prefer to use margarine rather than butter, choose one which is high in polyunsaturates.

Olive Oil Has the best flavour, and, in my opinion, is the healthiest oil. For economy, use a supermarket blend for frying (but not deep-frying) and a virgin olive oil for salad dressings.

Vegetable Oils Groundnut oil is particularly good for roasting and deep-frying; otherwise, use any polyunsaturated oil such as sunflower, corn, safflower or soya. Grapeseed is good, but expensive. Blended vegetable oil may not be polyunsaturated.

White Vegetable Fat/Vegetable Suet Now quite widely available, these are useful for some baking and for making vegetarian suet crust, Christmas puddings and mincemeat.

OTHER INGREDIENTS

Note: Some ingredients are described at the beginning of the relevant recipe sections; for instance, rice is at the beginning of the section on MAIN MEAL RICE DISHES, pasta precedes MAIN MEAL PASTA DISHES, and flour and sugar are at the beginning of BREAD, CAKES AND BISCUITS. Here are a few miscellaneous items which aren't covered elsewhere.

Breadcrumbs, Dried and Fresh These are used quite a lot in vegetarian cookery, to give body to concentrated proteins such as nuts.

For soft wholewheat breadcrumbs, crumble 2–3 days old bread, crusts removed, in your fingers, or pop pieces of bread in a liquidizer or blender. Grinding up left-over pieces of bread and putting them into a polythene bag in the freezer is not only a virtuously thrifty thing to do, if you can get round to it, it also means there's usually a supply of breadcrumbs to hand! (They can be used straight from the freezer.)

Dried breadcrumbs can be made by spreading slices of bread on a dry baking sheet and baking in a cool oven (150°C/300°F/Gas Mark 2) for an hour or so, or until crisp and dried out, then putting the pieces into a polythene bag and pulverizing with a rolling pin, or by putting them into a food processor or liquidizer. Store in an airtight tin. Alternatively, it's now possible to buy good dried wholewheat breadcrumbs.

Canned Tomatoes A useful, economical ingredient for vegetarian savouries and sauces. The Italian tomatoes have the best flavour.

Seaweed: HIZIKI, WAKAME and NORI Types of seaweed, extremely rich in nutrients, particularly iron, calcium and B vitamins. They can be bought from some health food shops and stockists of Japanese foods. To prepare hiziki and wakame, rinse, then simmer in water for a few minutes to soften it slightly. Remove the central stem from wakame and chop the seaweed. Wakame can be made into a good soup,

Mushroom and Sea Vegetable soup (page 25) and hiziki into a delicate salad (page 112) or added to vegetable mixtures and stir-fries. Nori is used dry, and is toasted first. Hold a sheet of nori above a gas flame or electric ring until it becomes crisp and crunchy, then crumble it over salads, stir-fries and cooked vegetable dishes for extra nourishment as well as a pleasant salty, tangy flavour of the sea.

Tahini/Sesame Cream A thick purée, rather like peanut butter, made from sesame seeds. Can be spread on bread or mixed with water or oil and flavourings to make toppings and dressings. I use it to make Hummus (page 27). I prefer a light or pale type when I can get it. Stir in the oil, which rises to the top, before using.

Tofu A white curd made from soya milk. This can be bought from health food shops and Japanese shops. A firm tofu, which slices well, is available, and also a softer textured one, in a vacuum pack — this soft tofu can be whizzed into dressings and dips, but the firm one is most useful for savoury use.

To make a salad dressing, mix soft tofu in a liquidizer with a little lemon juice or water, salt and pepper, chopped herbs or garlic or other flavouring. This can be used in place of salad cream or mayonnaise for vegans.

A dessert can be made by liquidizing soft tofu with honey and soft fruit, such as strawberries.

Drain the firm tofu, cut it into cubes, toss these in flour and fry them; or simply heat the cubes in some stock. Serve with soy sauce and Chinese-style vegetables; or add the cubes of tofu to vegetable stir-fries.

14. Cooking Processes

BAKING Cooking in the oven by dry heat, as with bread, cakes, and Baked Potatoes.

Baking Blind When a pastry flan case is baked without a filling. Some cooks put a piece of greaseproof paper and some dry beans in the flan case to prevent the pastry from rising. These are removed after 15 minutes, and the flan is baked for a further 5 minutes to crisp the base (I do not myself bother with the paper and beans — see page 94).

Basting Spooning oil or fat over food as it is roasting, as in the Lentil Roast on page 41.

Blanching Immersing food in boiling water for a brief time, to loosen the skins, as in tomatoes, almonds or peaches, or to destroy enzymes in food which is to be frozen.

Boiling Cooking food in boiling water.

Braising When food is cooked over a gentle heat, with just a little liquid and a lid on the pan, as described for Celery, on page 124.

Creaming When butter or margarine and sugar are beaten together until they are light and creamy. This incorporates air in the mixture to give a light texture to cakes.

Dropping Consistency The consistency of cake mixture when it will drop off the spoon within 5 seconds.

Folding In When ingredients are added to a creamed or whisked mixture without stirring too much, so that the air in the mixture is retained. Folding is done with a metal spoon, and the creamed or whisked mixture is lifted up over the new mixture, or 'folded' over it, until the two mixtures have been combined.

Frying Deep frying is when the food is fried by being immersed in hot deep fat or oil; shallow-frying is when the food is cooked in 3–5 cm/⅛–¼ inch of hot fat or oil in a frying pan, and turned as necessary, until cooked and browned all over.

Grilling When food is browned and cooked under the radiant heat of a grill.

Poaching When food is simmered gently in a pan without a lid.

Roasting Cooking food over an open flame or in the oven, with or without additional fat (as in Roast Potatoes, page 127).

Rubbing In Combining two ingredients, usually flour and fat, with the finger tips, using short, light movements, until the mixture looks like breadcrumbs, with no lumps of fat visible.

Sautéing Another term for shallow-frying.

Sieving Pushing food through a sieve to make a purée.

Sifting Shaking flour or other dry ingredients through a sieve to remove lumps.

Steaming Cooking food in the steam of boiling water.

Stewing Cooking food gently in simmering liquid, either in the oven or on top of the stove.

Stir Frying Frying food quickly in a little fat or oil, stirring all the time, until the food is heated through and lightly cooked. Food which takes longer to cook can be put in first, then other ingredients added. The food should be cut into smallish even-sized pieces which will cook rapidly.

Whipping/Whisking Beating a mixture vigorously with a whisk or fork to incorporate air.

15. Equipment

Good equipment saves time and effort and adds to the pleasure of cooking. When buying equipment, as with most things, you get what you pay for; it really is worthwhile taking time to build up a collection of best-quality items. These are the basics:

CUTTING AND GRATING EQUIPMENT

French Sabatier Knife, with a 13 cm/5 inch blade — be sure to get a genuine one, and buy a steel to sharpen it.

Knife with a Serrated Stainless Steel Blade, similar in size to the Sabatier, for cutting delicate fruits and vegetables which a steel knife can taint with a metallic taste.

Chopping Board, a solid wooden one, at least 2.5 cm/ 1 inch thick, and not less than 40 × 30 cm/16 × 12 inches (this can double as a pastry board, particularly useful for rolling out wholewheat pastry).

Kitchen Scissors, good sharp ones, useful for many jobs, including snipping fresh herbs.

Potato Peeler, the kind with a swivel blade.

Box Grater which you can stand on the chopping board to grate small quantities of carrot, etc.

Nutmeg Grater, some have a small compartment for storing the pieces of nutmeg.

Food Processor, not essential, but particularly useful. As with most good equipment, you'll use it more than you imagine possible, so get a big and strong one.

Electric Liquidizer/Coffee Grinder, a cheaper alternative to a food processor; it is useful (the liquidizer for blending soups and dips, and the coffee grinder for grinding nuts) but not as versatile as a food processor.

Handheld Rotary Grater, the cheapest way to grind nuts (and other items).

PANS, BOWLS, TINS AND CASSEROLES

Clear Glass Bowls, one large, a medium-sized one, a couple of small ones, would be a minimum, though more are always useful.

Pudding Basins, a 1.2 litre/2 pint one for making Christmas pudding; a 900 ml (1½ pint) for steamed syrup pudding, and 1½ litre (2½–3 pint) for steamed vegetable pudding.

Saucepans, heavy-gauge stainless steel are the best, I think, and last a lifetime. You'll need a large one — at least 2.75 litres/5 pints — for cooking pasta and stir-fries, plus a couple of medium-sized ones and a small one, all with lids.

Frying Pan, the ideal is to have more than one, in a range of sizes; one measuring 27.5/10¾ inches across, for general frying and 2-person omelettes, and one measuring 15 cm/5–6 inches across for 1-person omelettes and pancakes.

Pressure Cooker, not essential, but useful for soups and cooking pulses. If you buy a large stainless-steel one, the base can double as a saucepan for cooking pasta etc.

Casserole Dishes, one deep and big, at least 2.5 litres/4½ pints, with a lid, and a shallow casserole about 5 cm/2 inches deep, in a range of sizes; 19 × 29 cm/7½ × 11½ inches, 23 × 21 cm/9 × 8½ inches and 32 × 24 cm/12½ × 9½ inches. An ordinary round pie plate, 20–23 cm/8–9 inches, a 1 litre (1¾ pint) capacity pie dish with a rim, and a large round white pizza plate, 30 cm/12 inches across, are also useful.

Baking Tins. Buy good strong ones that won't buckle. A basic list would be: two or three baking sheets; two 450 g (1 lb) heavy bread tins, and a 900 g (2 lb) one; an 18 cm/ 7 inch and a 20 cm/8 inch deep round cake tin; a 20 cm/ 8 inch fluted flan tin with a loose base; a shallow bun tin with 12 sections (several of these, if you make lots of mincepies at Christmas, saves time); two shallow swiss roll tins measuring 16 × 28 cm/7 × 12 inches, and 25 × 35 cm/ 10 × 14 inches; and two 18 cm/7 inch sandwich cake tins; a 20 cm/8 inch spring-clip cake tin is useful if you like making cheesecakes, and can double as a round cake tin; 20 cm/8 inch round tin, for cakes like gingerbread.

MEASURING EQUIPMENT

Scales, robust ones, that you can keep out on the working surface, if there's room, or wall-fitted ones if space is scarce. I like the kind which have a large bowl and a dial that you can reset, so that you can weigh several ingredients on top of one another.

Measuring Spoons, a set of the standard ones: 15 ml/1 tablespoon, 10 ml/2 teaspoons, 5 ml/1 teaspoon and 2.5 ml/ ½ teaspoon.

Measuring Jug, a 1 litre (2 pint) heatproof opaque plastic jug, plus one or two clear glass measuring jugs 300 ml/½ pint) and 600 ml (1 pint) capacity, are always useful.

SPOONS, WHISKS,
SMALL PIECES OF EQUIPMENT

Wooden Spoons, in several sizes; I find a small flat one particularly useful.

Metal Spoons, a couple of tablespoons and several teaspoons.

Forks, one or two old forks.

Egg Whisk, a medium-sized balloon type, plus either a hand-held or electric rotary whisk.

Apple Corer, useful if you like baked apples, for taking out the cores in one piece.

Garlic Press, not essential, as you can always crush garlic on a board with the blade of a knife; but if you get a garlic press, buy a strong steel one with large holes.

Pastry Brush, a fat real bristle one.

Palette Knife

Fish Slice

Potato Masher

Can Opener, a wall-mounted one is the most convenient.

OTHER EQUIPMENT

Orange Squeezer, the type with a jug underneath to catch the juice.

Colander, metal, for draining pasta and vegetables, as well as doubling as a steamer if placed over a saucepan of boiling water.

Sieves, a large metal one for sifting flour, and one with nylon mesh for sieving fruits (without imparting a metallic taste).

Rolling Pin, a plain wooden one without handles, at least 4 cm/16 inches long.

Pastry Cutters, a set of round ones, measuring 5 cm/2 inches, 6 cm/2½ inches and 7.5 cm/3 inches.

Piping Bag, not essential, but useful for piping whipped cream or meringue (to make Pavlova, for instance), a nylon bag with a large and a medium-sized shell nozzle, or a selection of nozzles.

Pestle and Mortar, not essential, but useful for crushing spices.

Timer A timer on a rope, that you can hang round your neck when you leave the room, is useful.

INDEX

INDEX

Rose Elliot's

Vegetarian Fast Food

Are you short of time but need a tasty meal in minutes? *Rose Elliot's Vegetarian Fast Food* has over 200 recipes, all of which can be made in under half an hour!

Rose has combined ingenuity with speed to create mouth-watering, highly original meals in no time. Here is fast food for any occasion – from a quick solo snack, to a speedy lunch with a friend, or a last-minute impromptu supper.

Starting with the storecupboard, Rose gives valuable tips on what to have in stock to ensure you always have the basis of a quick meal or snack. Then, each of the next six chapters is based around key main ingredients: bread; eggs, cheese and dairy foods; pasta; pulses, grains and nuts; vegetables; fruit.

Each chapter is filled with delicious recipes that make use of everyday storecupboard items as well as fresh ingredients and treats for those special occasions.

Keep *Rose Elliot's Vegetarian Fast Food* handy in the kitchen – you'll never need to worry again when called upon to rustle up a quick meal.

Rose Elliot's

The Bean Book

Beans are an invaluable part of our diet, for not only do they provide an inexpensive source of protein, but they are rich in iron, phosphorous and B vitamins. Throughout history the bean has sustained generations, and here Rose Elliot's flair and inventiveness bring us a host of delicious recipes using more varieties of beans than you ever imagined existed.

Rose Elliot is Britain's top writer on vegetarian cookery and in this classic collection of original recipes the humble bean is utterly transformed. There are spicy dals from India; crisp, tasty rissoles; delectable pâtés and bean salads, shiny with dressing and fragrant with herbs. Delicate bean dishes from France, robust ones from Italy, others from the Middle East, with more than a hint of olive oil, lemon and garlic, full of earthy charm.

Vegetarian or non-vegetarian, nobody can resist Rose Elliot's imaginative and colourful dishes, a sheer delight to the palate and the eye.

Rose Elliot's

Vegetarian Christmas

Christmas is special: a time to reflect, to draw closer together as a family, a time to count your blessings and to celebrate them – and a time to eat!

In *Vegetarian Christmas*, Rose Elliot has written her most personal, most delicious book yet so that you, too, can create festive food that will truly help sustain that Christmas magic. Starting with the preparations (including invaluable freeze-ahead tips and recipes), *Rose Elliot's Vegetarian Christmas* features a whole host of family recipes to eat throughout the season.

At the heart of the book is a selection of six superb Christmas Day menus to make the big day a great success. The accent here is on celebration, on utter satisfaction guaranteed. And each menu comes complete with tips, advice and a specially constructed countdown to enable the cook to enjoy Christmas Day as much as the rest of the family.

Rose Elliot's Vegetarian Christmas, with its very special recipes and evocative photographs, ensures that vegetarians and non-vegetarians alike at last have a book that will give them the most superb and food-filled holiday ever. Happy eating!

Rose Elliot's

Not Just a Load of Old Lentils

Rose Elliot has long been one of Britain's top vegetarian cookery writers. Apart from being healthy, vegetarian food is delicious, tasty and colourful and Rose Elliot's many books are packed full with hundreds of creative and original recipes which appeal to everyone, vegetarians and non-vegetarians alike.

Not Just a Load of Old Lentils is a classic in the world of vegetarian cookery and has been a best-seller since it was first published. With more than 400 recipes covering everything from soups and starters through to desserts, cakes and biscuits it offers mouthwatering ideas for every taste and occasion.

For already devoted vegetarians Rose Elliot provides fresh inspiration, and the vitality and enthusiasm of her writing will send many a meat-eater rummaging through the vegetable racks.

'*Not Just a Load of Old Lentils* makes an impact from the first' – *Health for All*

Rose Elliot's

Vegetarian Four Seasons

Spring, summer, autumn and winter – each has its own special character and attractions, and food plays a major role in our enjoyment of these passing seasons. *Rose Elliot's Vegetarian Four Seasons* takes you on a culinary journey through the year, with a specially chosen collection of delicious recipes representing the culmination of her years of experience and her talent. Here are fresh, clean tastes in spring; cool, soothing flavours for hot summer days; mellow, rich dishes for autumn; and warming, hearty food to help keep out the winter cold.

The recipes range from superb soups and starters to mouth-watering desserts and puddings – with many marvellous main courses along the way. Each of the four chapters also includes some fabulous special occasion menus – a harvest supper for autumn, a party buffet for winter, a fresh-from-the-garden dinner for spring, and a family barbecue for summer, among others.

Rose Elliot's Vegetarian Four Seasons, with its spectacular recipes and evocative photographs, will help everyone – whether vegetarian, non-vegetarian, vegan or food combiner – to gain a special something from the passing months, and to enjoy the happiest food-filled year ever.

THE BEAN BOOK	0 7225 3043 9	£5.99	☐
VEGETARIAN CHRISTMAS	0 00412 681 5	£14.99	☐
NOT JUST A LOAD OF OLD LENTILS	0 7225 3037 4	£5.99	☐
VEGETARIAN FOUR SEASONS	0 00412 913 X	£14.99	☐
VEGETARIAN COOKERY	0 00412 681 5	£14.99	☐
COMPLETE VEGETARIAN COOKBOOK	0 00412 009 4	£12.99	☐
SUPREME VEGETARIAN COOKBOOK	0 00063 757 3	£7.99	☐
MOTHER AND BABY BOOK	0 7225 2993 7	£4.99	☐

All these books are available from your local bookseller or can be ordered direct from the publishers.

To order direct just tick the titles you want and fill in the form below:

Name: _____

Address: _____

_____

_____ Postcode: _____

Send to: Thorsons Mail Order, Dept 3, HarperCollins*Publishers*, Westerhill Road, Bishopbriggs, Glasgow G64 2QT.
Please enclose a cheque or postal order or your authority to debit your Visa/Access account —

Credit card no: _____

Expiry date: _____

Signature: _____

— to the value of the cover price plus:
UK & BFPO: Add £1.00 for the first book and 25p for each additional book ordered.

Overseas orders including Eire: Please add £2.95 service charge. Books will be sent by surface mail but quotes for airmail despatches will be given on request.

24 HOUR TELEPHONE ORDERING SERVICE FOR ACCESS/VISA CARDHOLDERS — **TEL: 041 772 2281.**